COLLECTED POEMS

Anne Ridler

COLLECTED POEMS

CARCANET

First published in 1994, second edition 1997 by
Carcanet Press Limited
4th Floor, Conavon Court
12–16 Blackfriars Street
Manchester M3 5BQ

A CIP catalogue record for this book
is available from the British Library.
ISBN 1 85754 317 3

The publisher acknowledges financial assistance from the
Arts Council of England.

Set in 10pt Palatino by Bryan Williamson, Frome
Printed & bound by Antony Rowe Ltd, Eastbourne

For Vivian

Foreword

Most of these poems are reprinted from seven collections, namely: *Poems* (Oxford University Press, 1939); *The Nine Bright Shiners* (1943), *The Golden Bird* (1951), *A Matter of Life and Death* (1959), *Some Time After* (1972), *New and Selected Poems* (1988), all published by Faber and Faber; and *Selected Poems* (Macmillan, New York, 1961). To these I have added a few poems written since the 1988 collection or not included there, and a section called 'Words for Music', with texts reprinted from *Some Time After* (Faber, 1972), *The Jesse Tree* (The Lyrebird Press, 1972), and *A Passion Cantata* (Roberton Publications, 1993). I have also included the choruses from my play, *The Trial of Thomas Cranmer* (Faber, 1956).

Many of the poems were first printed in periodicals and anthologies; some have been broadcast by the BBC; and some are available on a cassette with commentary, made by Norwich Tapes Ltd.

I have retained the order of the poems published in book form, except for the first book, of early poems. Here I have altered the order to make it more nearly chronological, as was the order in the other books. Here too I have made a few verbal changes, which reflect my original versions (first altered to follow suggestions which I now think were for the worse).

A.R.

Contents

In Cornwall

Westward where the cliff falls
In dark walls through Cornish seas still haunted
By drowned men who shoulder toward the land,
By grim mermaids and the pained cry of gulls,

I have seen, on fine days
Lying lazy, when all this seemed innocent
(And while I watched, the lemon-coloured tide,
That wrinkles like a melting jelly, rose

To the pale mark on sunburnt rock),
I have seen the flicker of light far out on bayonets –
Winking above the wave – of a submerged army
That waits its time. But a cloud sweeps them back

Into an endless milky sea
That seems the bright and easy floor of heaven:
Like heaven that will not let the earth remain
In sin, but grinds its outworks endlessly,

And steals up its shore
With power hidden in the surf's feeling finger.
There saints like ships can navigate, and fair
The crops of golden plants like sparkles shine.
And O that we were there.

Shooting of his Dear

With my love swiffling round me, I took her to be a swan,
and I shot my dear darling with a ratteling gun.

Of all the valiant who visited that tower,
   Not one knew enough to tell him.
His mild retainers rose at an early hour,
   Twenty, ten red-, ten black-complexioned:
And they drenched their beards in cream,
For he liked to see them sleek, and their liveries gleam.

This was their only luxury: all the day
      They worked to keep the castle running,
The brazen gates and the rose-garden gay.
      The stone medallions shone with health,
And the gold griffin from the western wall
At sunset lit the loiterers down the hill.

The polished summer days should have been pleasant,
      But another day, years past, had spoilt them.
He was then young, and loved a girl as constant
      As gentle as himself; but though
He knew himself beloved, he could not
Quite forgive the pain of love in his heart.

The sense of his unworthiness half drowned him,
      First learnt by love, and with the fear,
Palpitant, of her death, did so surround him,
      Resentment toward her mixed with love;
Though he in all unconsciousness
Thought that he blamed his abject heart for his distress.

By the lake behind the tower, one autumn day,
      He walked, his practical reason
To shoot the swans, too numerous there. The grey
      And chilly earth raised clouds so low
They seemed the white-feathered strange birds swooping,
And the sound of the unseen water, their beaks dipping.

The acrid air was swan-swept, and the sky
      Shrieked with them, when from white gloom stepped
His sweetheart, hoping to surprise him, and shy.
      He paused, then fired, and she fell.
Instant comfort filled his being:
He had done what they needed, and saw her dead, unseeing.

He turned to lift her up, and then only
      Realised she would not walk again;
And for such another he could search the world vainly.
      Had he killed her knowingly, or
Shot her for a swan? But more than this
He was worried, in lifting her, by her staring eyes.

They said he had thought her, coming in the mist, a swan.
He could not be sure; but if he had known her –
This doubt murdered him, year upon year again –
Why had he shot, and why felt joy
And extreme appeasement? She was his dear,
He loved her, and the antinomy was more than he could bear.

Yet of all the valiant who visited that tower,
Not one knew enough to tell him.
He did not marry, but let the comfortable hours
Of a safe life in a pleasant place
Swathe him unhealing, till one night –
He with his griffin and his men in the firelight –

Perhaps the bird spoke, or perhaps merely
Now that he knew his life, and was old,
At last he looked into his own depth clearly.
He knew he had killed her, and knew why.
His own misery was on her head,
Her burden: he could not love until this was dead.

And he had made no attempt at understanding
How she had but the one life,
And killed, for the blatant beast, his own darling.
But that it had been done in blindness
The quick with the dead could reconcile,
And an incorruptible love unfurl.

In a Wood

All things quick, all brightness has a damp mist doomed;
Chill trees smother the night-sick ground;
The slick moon creeping down the boughs died drowned;
I hear my heart rap, dead, distant, as a miner deep entombed.

My torch-beam but proves, as the hopefulness of questing mind,
Tangle of phenomena, all's diffused.
O vague shapes, take definition, as first
The spring in its clarity of leaves, while I apprehend

How from my treasure the City lights love-driven shine,
   Streets spread wide from his footsteps, reared
   From his thoughts are houses; and so reassured
Let belief bring his heart-beats livening the darkness and mine.

Fathers that their Children Loved

'Fathers that their children loved, that died and left them
See how forlorn, since the world began,
Have had, their bones once crumbled, the sad children
Make sugar out of them, feed their hearts to be man.

You make as you move, new moons for old.'
This is the old tipster, who snores inside the heart
Till its distress, and then comes up with comfort –
A reflex rise, for despair would lose him his cot.

What good to me now to know that I shall forget?
Parents and those I loved and took for guide,
I can see you but not touch over these forty years
That stole my march, promised me pain ere I was made.

For when you die I may do very well for myself,
But things can no more be known with your mind,
And the fresh event must go maimed; I chase
Those years now in my youth, and must to the end.

Christ took off his coat of flesh and left a sight
Smites down lids with brightness: now could I catch
On my eye such shaft, be luculent with your light
Entirely, dying should never cancel the touch.

For a London Boy

Now for a boy in London wishing a life,
Through commons of childhood, ways known to be safe,
See the paths, plot in the asphalt precincts
Parallels with the country child to please him.
Woods white and blue, smoky with bluebell and cherry,
Fume of anemone curling rarely, carry
To murkier smoke but soft, sleep for the sun;
Sunday fields sober for pasture feeding
To churchward pavements stiff to bear his treading,
Merry for hop-scotch; morning hooter's blare
For stamping rabbit, maddening cuckoo, hear –
Hint of restriction coming. May he the wiser
See what freedom he can, quick as professor
Spying with glass birds in the dense glade.
May in his mind the sceptic and the poet
Grow, and though he have discomfort from it,
May his disquiet end with belief found,
Stability honest, and secure his mind.

Old Goose of Time

Old goose of Time bearing sons over spate,
Taxi faring northward in the night,
This man having for your peregrination,
Since he may not be let stop still in one station –
Never still in my arms – carry him with conscience,
Knowing what you take: the Lord Almighty's precious,
The luck of Holiness, and to the earth,
To beggars, the wish we can ride on, to me my mind's life.
Car which from the given kiss always the presence takes,
As Time him from his present – which he cries to leave or likes
But never moans after – seize him now sweetly:
Not for any nonsense of a five-score sprightly
And brown locks unsilvered, but bring him to the silver
The splendour of his life, that has no past or future

Yet both, the wink of which dumbs my desire.
So then you can take him, I'll not cry after him,
Even wishing to, my dandy, my fire
And phalanx of words against the crying demon;
Bring him to his fine, excellent peace in heaven.

The Car at Night

The Dragon that our Seas did raise his Crest...

ROBERT HAYMAN

Walking in darkness the welt of the world
Where the blurred trees lace it from the turning of space,
I saw my frame foreshortened creep upon its crust,
Legs bandy as a man's are, spotted from a tower,
A mere moving animal; indeed I despaired
Of descending to wake it, my floating observer
Warm in the skin, when as at a bell
The land thrilled; not at my tread it trembled,
Waiting like a nervous guest, its rim flushed with light.
What beast from the bracken might plunge, or plashing
Through the air dripping with stars could crest the sleep
Of the deep-drenched world? wondering met me with my body,
Remembering the dinosaur, ichthyosaurus,
That did not awake from that sleep of the numb crust
Like the manageable prodigies bred in our age.
The light climbed the curved world, the driven dragon came.

Our mild air scorches his lip, self-corroding his throat burns,
Uncooled by his water, though here the leaves whisper
Smooth my pricking heart, his speed is his fire:
Our kind day's dragon, a pelican peer,
Feeds only on himself, whose going makes green crystal caves
The trees above, red danger signs the birds' eyes,
And pale lights the deer's, pinking out his path,
That die as he passes, blind as a black-out.
Now quiet, now sleep, like snails, crawl from crevices,
Smear in seeming the world to primeval
Nervelessness again, and I to the west
Make after the far light, the dragon's crest.

The Crab

The crab is in again, his monthly house
Open and loth, patient only of force;
Here he huddles on my back, the pools
That three weeks hid him, after the queasy pale
Swept up my path before him, washed him to me.
Kings feeding fat, clogged rivers on the plain,
Or choked with stars the dark, as all satiety
I feel him, clutching there, while each capacity
Goes to enlarge him; dance the pincers of pain,
My self flies rook up to watch, afraid of the din,
Sings to cover it, yet hears and rooted feels.

Any day beats by, force accepted, heals
Nightly homing the Monday gloom of an office –
If you can say it heals that turns from brass
Bitter to stealing hope in the mind a knowledge
In facts unchanged. So as with the anxious,
This wasteful process can seem gentle to us,
Flown out in peace all the disgust of blood and illness.
For we take comfort in any achievement, even a courage
That could not be refused: this inner success
May weight circumstance to temporary peace.
Even the periodic cancer need not distress us,
Could we but keep the peace and lose the venomous.

Against Anger

The boy asking – in a swing travelling to the moon
Through curled ice of the spinney frozen with flowers –
'The bery old man on the moon, does he wear a beret?'
The poet in the glassy office doorway,
Unable to remember the Professor's Christian name;
And the man I love, in another glass
Seeing his looks of delight as an unlikeable face
And his eloquence as a hum, surprised at our prizing,
Had such humility I think they cannot be wounded,

Their unmeant sweetness makes them a safe place.
Next when I kill him in my heart for harms
I think he does me, and when next am raging,
This remembering, let it save
My mind from the hell-go-round of the grievance-ridden,
Save the fool turkey-cock into love.

In the Sea

My soul in the oily sea unmoved lay
    Either by dark ruffle of mackerel or
The fear of watchers on the cliff, who see
    When waves crash their helpless bodies there:
    A curious death, with the safe land near
And the sight so lovely, to die in cream,
Yet how certain, in that maelstrom.

I lay fathoms deep, turned not my eyes
    To Lundy east and the seal's sarcastic laugh,
Nor west where Trevose in these glittering fields lays
    His flat head, and we see water over his coif,
    Nor near at hand where waves clutch the cliff,
Throwing back ropes of white foam torn apart;
Never stirring for them, for fear of hurt,

Determined at all costs to be buried from sadness.
    But my excitable love waking soon
Whipped up the dusk storm, sent me rudderless
    In a whirling winter, towards the shore ran,
    Was circles of foam round me, was dragging moon:
Till not Ulysses, by the relenting sea
Thrown gently on the beach, more helpless came than I.

The Drunken Air yet Thirsty
In Memoriam Peter Burra, killed in a plane crash on solo flight

The drunken air yet thirsty,
The brooding god grasping you, my beauty,
As he found you in his tower, your looks hid
Though in leather and glass to prove your manhood,
He knew and would prove your double nature,
And the dreadful crash proved you mortal creature.

Death at six and twenty,
If we expect purgation and eternity
And trust your dolphin leap from the chance of hell,
Leaves us to howl at long life, but why to feel
This that will not grow quieter,
The dinning pity at heart for you, dead Peter?

Is it for frustration
Of all your plans and promise, the remission
Never to be made for the big work put off?
No, for had you written out a long life
The end would have seemed a lost pledge;
Whatever the joy, the sorrow must have been huge.

Not that, but the cataclysm
Of start so sudden into a new heaven
Or death, and because you did not mean it;
That the Lord should gird you, not in your decrepit
But in your youth, huddled
To death with the letter in the car unposted.

That living letter death's reporter
Turned to me, and I who now mutter
A flat requiem, have no right to grieve,
Not being sister, benefactor nor your love,
Only at a friendship's entrance, now
Not early enough begun, but yet I do.

May, when the shock is over,
Your lovely knowledge make you a safer cover
And stronger wings than the traitor plane had:
Skill in the dimensions of colour sound and word,
Skill in gentleness, make
You in the spheres of perfection neither ignorant nor desolate.

Red Sea in the City

I came one morning down to where he waits,
Watched him walk presenting all the streets
As lucky moons with light, and saw the sad
Since east-wind colour in his grey suit saved.
Traffic waves checked as he crossed the road
(Who flattered Canute here were justified).
It is loving-kindness mortalised to mind
Makes grey merry and fixed laws attend.
With this he now learns divinity's play,
Setting to-day in the City the Red Sea,
Whose talking cuts our cackling race in two
And piles up speech to wait while his goes by,
Walking, in grey so suitable to joy,
Made solids water, water a wall to his way.

From the Theme of
O Hush Thee, my Baby

O hush, be my honey,
    Your forehead is bright,
But the Three Noble Guardians
    Are pleasant to-night;
    Have mercy to-night.

Gloved is their steel hand
    Their hundred eyes kind,
O cloud in its curved sheath
    The moon of your mind;
    No god will mind.

Where walks on the water
    And on horseback rides
The wisher, all poets
    Speak pearls, never toads,
    So fresh are their words;

Where drudges drink cream,
  You'd wish as much as I
To kiss, and my heart be
  The apple of your eye,
  Your apple I.

In that pretty crystal
  To get one's wish is peace;
A heaven, but looked at
  In the looking-glass,
  Oneself in the glass.

Kiss the glassed face;
  But where it was kissed
The third holy Guardian
  Lifts his mailed fist,
  Lightning of the Ghost.

Hush us, my hero
  From singing for our fate,
Beam us to silence
  With an unsheathed light,
  Your forehead be bright.

Cold in March

The cutting voice of tits in trees
  Scissors out the tunnelled spring,
While hangs for airing in the breeze
  Its leaf and catkin new linen.

Sunday cars come bagging gold
  To pollen cheapened walls in town,
Too gaudy for the withered field
  That keeps its frosty nightcap down.

I, like the icebound air
  That stutters through the chaffy stalks,
Cough and sneeze, the signs of fire
  Through house of glass wherein I walk

See unwarmed, and guess the scents
    My membrane deaf as wool debars,
A one-eyed wisher of new mints
    Of life my griffin sense obscures.

Let creature once again seem noble
    Sir, and let that be soon,
For soon we find cold and trivial,
    What we throve and took fire on.

The Rudiment is Single

So varied the world, the rudiment is single:
    Here lunacy lies in the house the scientists build.
Wind-fluid fields and marbled sea so tangle
    Knowledge, we would not swear our steps earth-held
In eddying grass or sea-borne, yet to survive
Keep seeming under, and choose what we'll believe.

In Cornwall, where the sea is stolen land,
    Though long digested, changed so that no tree
Roots by our cables groping through that sand
    Except by our speech unstirred since the break away,
And the litter of lithic man no dustman clears,
Easy to confuse the elements and years.

A man coming in sunlight and sharp wind
    Down the moors, his heart cold and crazed
With life gone wrong, saw at the road's end
    – Passing centuries – a plain, and on it spaced
(Where rocks raised smoking spray) bonfires, and moved
There for warmth, while round him the hills heaved.

That sea lay solid, stained with shadow of cloud,
    Brown and green, lit by the flare of gulls;
The high grass raced towards him and he fled
    Fearing a chasing tide, and left the hills,
Saw flame where spray met sunbeams, and being wild
Held his hands to the waves to warm his cold.

Cried that the fire leapt, it scorched him, ran
For dangerous comfort to the frosty glass
Where granite ground the water to white and green.
The sea broke in his head, the burning ice
Received him, and the scarp of salt devoured;
And he in earth air fire or water dazzled and died.

Dialogue between Three Characters and a Chorus

CHORUS

In old Moralities could be included
The entire structure of the world; we bound
To audit for a less rich philosophy
Add meagre figures, note
Tentative conclusions. Heart's problems
So little we think can touch on, little know,
Deciding were absurd.
Yet the delightful then as now dissolving –
Cloud-clarity quick to the unhappy mists –
Denied their daily joys eternal,
Which man for that the more firmly believed.
We also, less inclusive,
Try so to state our world's stability.
And while this Catherine wheel of poetry,
Firing its dark-defying sparks, whirls,
Allow its impetus, not for a beacon
This quasi-Morality, but a mind's show.

This mind, from its several forms
Speaks first in an unconfident fantasy of love.

THE YOUNG MAN

As white is she
And to my touch as choice and briefly satisfactory
As whitebeam leaves that the wind whips aloft,
Which tell to the eye their texture soft,
Sweet message sent
To fingertips, and sweetness quickly spent.

Where she goes
Sliding curtains of the rain on rods of sun her ways enclose,
River-whirling gulls her gay sky receives,
Roads, their hostile posters furled,
Bless with arching eaves;
She my love by London gentled as by space the spinning world.

That's all very well indeed,
But not the girl I love.
Yet, did the tallies fit of what's flesh and what image,
I through my image could never meet the girl.
For what's created is gone out of us,
No aspirin for our pain of impermanence,
Since at the moment of its birth
Comes this tediously repeated separation;
We are gone in our flux,
Never to know it as at the moment of conception.
Yet I still spend myself with writing poems,
By that pleasure – being never more to kiss her –
Trying to order my disordered loss.
Needs little to account for the strange suffering of love:
Union is wild against possibility,
Wild as the winter-burning sky
Wishing to change its cold separate lights to the sun.
Yet, lasting union being denied,
Scattered as stars, what can fix us, lonely?
The giddy poles of the physical earth,
Its night-fields for covering?
We, strange to our changing selves, and our works grown
        strangers,
Whirling forlorn.

THE GIRL

I heard you, but am unable to speak
My opinion, or to recount my plight.
Words are weapons too heavy for my holding,
The dearest, the worst. Blades that should cut the mystery,
Wavering, hurt myself. I am so uncertain
Speaking – forced to – I watch for the scorn hidden
In the clear coherent answers of my friends.
I am frightened; how when my mind's best strength,

Reeling in clouds and dizzy, is weak to grasp
And grasping cannot hold even one thought
Steady and firm for analysing, how
Shall I ever govern all the terrible powers
Which beat on my senses, or do the difficult things
My life requires of me? O and its length lies out
Say fifty years, that's how many million minutes
Of painful pulse-beats? length is insupportable
In the exhaustion of fear . . . unless I died . . .
What a hope! for it seems the frightened never die,
Always can bear it, though their minds be sundered
From all sanity, all confidence, hurled,
Missing the ladder of logic, into a void.
Sir, since you spoke with knowledge, even of misery,
Hold me from falling, teach my mind to be logical,
To find its safety against the enormous world;
Tell me if my own selfhood will bring me strength.

THE YOUNG MAN

Let us assume the facts of you and I –
Premise hard to define, assume we know it –
And a chaos round us not so ordered as Milton's
Which we endure, less movable than his Fiend.
Now you and I, being young, even portentous,
Cannot define the causes of our pain,
Perhaps are racked for nothing,
And being causeless cannot move in the Night.

Control is by definition;
And consider how the Son of God, how even Saint Paul,
Their God a *consuming fire*, consumed the world,
The antinomical, in a defined rational peace.
My yoke is easy; We die daily;
Are facts inimical, phrases locked in truth.
For us, laughter is a kind of definition,
Knowing the separate incongruous facts
(Whence our pain, it is true).
This might be a weapon, a hope for balance,
This and the burning dangerous poise of words.

Permanence and poise!
Permanence wished for a putrefying fish
Poised out there in the scum-stream, cuttlefish
Cuttlefish and kettledrum, clanging your harp
Strummed in the gutter-muck, much lost
Yes much scarred by my scorning.
Do I want permanence of cuttlefish decaying?
Less then wish it of my sanguinary self:
My Self, so loaded with qualities, beringed with your rhymes
Fur-coated with your love, love's dowager, doomed
To perpetual receiving, smiling, never can give
Nor sacrifice nearly as much as she has;
Mind like a mimsy Christmas tree,
No lights native, smirking with tinsel of self-consciousness.
Take some other religion, and leave me
Until I give as you to me. Then
In a close dark with lids no longer pierced
By tearing brightness beating from the myths
In flight around me, system of your sky,
Eyes inset, I'll use my ears, sound
Of my own time beating hark to. Beats there
In no less common grief than yours this sense
Of present actuality, for hearts
Beggar-stabbed in every street, half wishing
To lose all if it might remedy, and jostled
By senseless haste of life, cooled in faith
Of physical tenderness, daily good of friends
Also healing, see in these phenomena
Meaning and mystery enough, disclaim
The supernatural. Such states of soul
As in a blear cloud sidling round the sun
Banished with beams, seen, or thickening buds
Of trees in town floodlit by lamps, splashed
Lavishly over a black sky, find secret
Suggested though not known of world's coherence;
Or in detachment after being ill,
Thrilled perception of peace. If these are visions,
Pasted up to illustrate religion
They give such pain because they passed as they,
Treated as transitory, would never wreak.

THE YOUNG MAN

Nobody but a fool would ever bring
Such states to prove his Deity;
Because an intellectual not a moody thing is a faith.

THE YOUNG WOMAN

But let me show you a vision of permanence:
Never say our twentieth century lacks it.
Come when the punctual hooter calls to see
The sharp machines in any factory;
Let your eyes fast on bright phalanx of steel,
Ignore the astral face above the wheel
Hovering, for the looks of boredom change
In the white guardian faces, but the range
Of the machine is constant, iron its jaws
Exactly crush the biscuits which had flaws,
Or tough bars dissolve into measured fire –

CHORUS

But I show you these visions with a different interpretation:
To understand them needs the acute and digestive mind of the
    theologian.
To no scolopendrae from the waters, monoceros, imaginations of
    man,
But to his intellectual scope pray, display us an Almighty.
Civilisation as engine starved expelling
Quick explosions bursts for the time of God;
These are dictatorships and torture. Now
See where those river-blazing signs borrow
Strength for unimportant message
From power of generated light and symbols
That once managed the mood of the varying year –
As lion snatched for beer, virgin for hair-wash,
And the magnificent rampant bull's fierceness
Condensed to meat-cubes; heavenly batteries
Might fix then to your daily lives to drive
And stabilise. These burning signs were once
Zodiac headlands in waters of the sky
Where the labouring sun steered; now is the sky
Creamy with floodlight whipped from the bowl of the town,
And constellations change to the earth, inverted

Now the Fish of the last house lies here,
And city-dimpled with dancing lights and dirt
These waters steer, turning the mystic and common,
Passing the points of your essential life.

Circled gasometers the mind knows fixed,
Yet to the sight pause ready for a touch
To start them wheeling, plot with equal points
Solid figures in the amenable blue
Your new Zodiac, plan of life. Power is about you
(So near you could disclaim the supernatural),
Myths are valid, old and new is irrelevance,
And yet to each his faith is new.

There are myths from data of your life
Sterile and fierce, crab-greediness, goat's decay,
Or green productive: will you hate what you are,
Or working with patience and pity even with yourselves
Be inclined to happiness?

The world moves, those that join this journey
Can travel by most houses of experience,
Intelligent and compassionate to pass with,
For pity is help, not dropping tears from a tower.
If now springs activity now know it
As one and three, for wherever the world tends –
Crash coming or the finger of God
Cancelling to new life, at least salvation
Is for the single yet not alone.

> Man sees poles of the known world
> On axis of his own heart moving;
> From it the yawning afternoon
> And the east-wind morning,
> Evening accidie stale with tears
> Slant away by the will are turning.

And severance of time from time might be mended,
Pity not decay the heart, useless, nor mind
Stonewall itself inactive, regretting impermanence.
And angry wishes might find quietus
Not in rigidity, not in divorce, but peace.

The Peacock and the Crane

Fine to a field of habit the peacock came:
  Where the wind mixed colour and seed
Prismatic, its broken fires made changing beam.
  Grey to that gleam the crane fed,
A night's thought mad in the day, strange from water its home.

Plunged its neck as down cool genuine wave,
  Spearing in shadows the worms for fish.
Amazing they stood; vanished; now I have
  No proof if they were incarnate wish,
Thoughts that imperative seem flesh, or really alive.

Though man could wring such blazing birds from air,
  Make thought take shape, the hope's wild.
So quick loving his kind, so kind aware
  Of known despair he still, though healed,
Makes nothing from his love will their despairing cure.

On being Asked for Pardon

Pardon implies a sin; then is it one
Not to be steel whenever the magnet is fain?
  Though wood as mad means prison,
Wood to unwished love is only sane.

Did you ask pardon for all gentle things
Said, and poetry and constant life? Such wrongs
  Should heal what wrongs caused madness,
And me, who with my pain reward them as sins.

Though I'll not cry you into crime, tears
Are here for some cause; it appears
  Heart's trials are illegal,
And will for nothing done accuse and curse.

Limbs have a grievance being uncoveted,
And mind an anger at its new growth of pride.
  O free me from fury,
Mend with your own forgiveness mine denied.

A Birthday

Lovers wishing to be one, so distant you see
  Lights but not the house, whom Plato excused
By a myth of primal joining, and who know
  What the mind promised to find the mood refused,
Who hold in each other a Proteus, and are baffled with
    politeness –
Help me now, where I wish to praise and bless,

To know what it is I would praise, would bless: dear
  And a man, and that which justifies the world
In its absurd gamble to be good. But where
  On the cumulus of his huge being piled
Could I find the place where the essential lies,
Or the night of making in the mature eyes?

Years behind his journey; only I discern
  Islington bow toward Saint Paul's, from when
Its tumbling children were distinguished. Born
  Crossing the Virgin's territory, who is his own
Where most he takes and gives, and grew slowly
In a whirlwind of words to scepticism and mercy.

And spoke of myths as living; and brought in
  The word *ineluctable*; and young could suffer,
As older he was brought into desperate pain
  But did not cease to love, and for ever –
Even unhappy – is forth from that narrow and steep,
In loving kindness no diviner can tell its scope.

Poetry makes a prickly crown, but he
  Has crowns more easy from his salvaged household;
I, cut by his voice from the cat's cradle of accidie
  And from worse despair, see on his birthday threshold
The drive of majesty – its gravel my joys
Of rocky hair and salamander eyes,

His hands that flame from the arm like Aaron's stick
  Changeable against the rest – and hear his heart
Knock so gently to tell the world's luck
  It lives. Let then this little be a taken part,
Useful a handle to offer the Lord Almighty,
Whereby to turn our blessing to felicity.

In Italy (1937): I

Seen from this littoral of the lake,
Its water that with the light was armour, soft
And sleek is now to the pricking drops of rain,
That make their tiny pits and die,
While the custard element the dolphins spurn.

I, on the cobb like tight-rope seeing
The umbrella-walkers, the pocket Mussolini
Approving the squads of trout, as accidents see
Them fallen on the essential grey,
Divisions devouring each other, lake and sky.

As lake and sky, the mind devours
The heart – whether as cannibal food, a change
Fruitless as in lower Hell, I could not know
Till I understood identity
And difference, and the doctrine of the Trinity.

The mind devours – inimical
To peace – what the heart must hold of guilt
For the pain you have in me, since it knows well
Its own lewd wishes, peacock's tail
Spread for the air, not you, but a spread snare.

I did not wish you a spear in the heart,
Self outgone for a girl, yet I did prank
And wish to be loved best, and now my friend
Have brought to harm; thus devour
Mind, heart, beneath the incidence of Italy.

Send the cypress temples, quiet
Croon of work from afar when one is idle,
Boy's voice tri-toned like the oleander,
Or sharp of hill on water, would
These comfort you, save me from grey devouring?

Landscapes echo, not convert
The mind, even Catullus' lake, and mine
Shows a merging monster; to make him a god
The triplicating passion needed
Flies like a high summit while we climb.

In Italy: II

In a green tree-crypt sleeping lay
The boy, who from his English day
Brought to the steel and silky lake,
Courted its colours while he woke,
Fled them asleep; through his head
Shot spears of cypress, drowned his bed
The moving streams of olive, down
Grey to the burnished lake, and pain
Its far blue to his tender eye.
The orange rocks had a cruel dye,
Dreadful the mountains' crystal scarp
As that which turned the prince's hope
To a slippery foothold, since he there
Was not fly to reach his dear.

The landward pools held possible peace,
The metal bent to a dark tress;
But stretching in his glittering sleep
For the fig-tree's carved unchanging shape,

The boy saw with charmed eyes
Dark from the lake a monster rise,
Scaled and with gaping jaws bloody,
Whom in endless chase of glory
Orlando met, and to slay was forced
Enter the throat in dangerous draught,
And conquered from inside. His fight
Was now renewed for the boy's sight,
While castle-high the waves were hurled,
The golden weeds uprooted whirled
To trap the sleepy snakes, and bled
Blue shore-flowers rent to red.

Kind and translucent rose the mountain
At sunset, like a strict guardian
Likeable at parting, his worry past;
Still they fought, and the form vast,
More terrible as more dim, grew
To hold a meaning the boy knew.
Colour-haunted sleep and gloom
From childhood dreaded to see this come:
The self devouring self, a strife
Private in his heart to find life
In the visible world. Now he saw;
But hiding his eyes in extreme woe
He could not see Orlando walk
Victor from fanged hell, and black
The monster sink, the water calm,
Silver for night, and stars give balm
To the broken plants; but crying there
Saw damnation and despair.

In Italy: III

Hovers the hawk towards the blue mountain,
Bearing on flat wings the fainting
Deadened gasp of guns in a mock war;
And now in caves as this where I perch for pleasure,
Men escape the brighter wings and smother
In their own sin and ours, and Italians cheer.

The sweet black-eyed boy and the friendly stranger,
Charming waiter, cheer, no stronger
To deny that what is three times told is the truth
Than I have been a hundred times, though horror
Takes me here for their blindness, where I see clearer.
But the crane of Europe's pain swings to a youth,

Where you sit, and perhaps weep, and wonder
The time, and will not look, that kinder
Passage to-day may bless you when you do;
And I see those tanks of hours come creeping
Too tardily up the hill, like the clouds' shadowing
On windless days, and your hope uncertain when they go.

If your precocious love left mine a seed,
He needs water and air to aid
His sleepy growth, and he needs constant pains,
To coax him up, and force him on with pleasure.
Only wait, and the matured treasure
Shall root and flower in you, and earn your sun.

London Summer

Pleasing girls now go in flounces,
    Green leaves slash the smart black trees,
And cheerful hopes of summer chances
    Prick the unlucky, unloved, to praise.

Pillows laze in the firmament,
    But summer pants stick to the thighs,
And pants the town in its winter paint,
    Blind our sight its burning eyes.

How useless our wish for the white wave broken,
    Whose traffic streams are all our tide,
And flowery hats a sufficient garden;
    Our nerves restless, with pleasure paid.

The Fancy and the True

The lovely dark one with the dandy face,
Harnessed star that speaks with gentle voice,
Neat birds to dovetail with our passions –
These are the dreams that with his hammer Love
Shall break to atoms.

The error of Narcissus was not vanity
So much, I imagine, as that he
Would have his dream the truth: loving, our dreams
Must die if we're to live, but that of the self is
Nothing but ashes.

Gazing at the glory, after a while
We turn to find our self, and find it vile,
That was so pretty and pleasant to live by.
It is nothing till our lover's sight
Takes up our eye.

Winter that salts the stars and gives the trees
Their marble hands, cannot our love freeze
That in cold came to its first bed.
Do not you then freeze in your own loss,
But take the house of your seen self from me,
Believe it true.

Why if cradled in your mother's pain,
Why if taught and nurtured in your own,
Did your hands and voice learn simplicity?
To lose to the irresponsible lucky? Rather
To gain your glory.

Bunhill Fields

Under cool trees the City tombs
    Extend, and nearer lie
Stones above Blake's and Bunyan's bones
    To Vivian's working days than I.

Since he is gentle, wild and good
    As you were, peaceable Shades,
There may he go within your care
    As in my heart his love resides.

Such a care as held unharmed
    The three within the fire;
Spread wings like those that led
    Tobias in the dangerous shire.

And if I fear his death too much,
    Let me not learn more faith
By sad trial of what I dread,
    Nor grieve him by my own death.

For our faith is one which may
    Convert but not console:
We shall not, except by our own will,
    Part for ever in the gape of hell.

At Christmas

Goe see the angry kynges.
                    JASPER HEYWOOD

Littered now the streets with light,
    Tiddler's ground of gold and silver;
        But we pass the free grotto,
    Pass the painter
        Chalking out our Christmas motto,
Till our present comes in sight.

Present time, though time's our gift.
　Before the delectable joys,
　　Before the kind kings appear,
　These to our eyes,
　　Thrones fierce and mean, show entire
The princedoms that our labours lift.

Their nursery faces much the same:
　Moloch with a dummy crown,
　　Of our rage the real dragon,
　The ape of pain;
　　These monuments of our private passion
As public tyrants have the blame.

Bombs will not bring removal.
　But You who take the same journey
　　As at this time, who seeing make
　Them unseen, may
　　Make unreal their dreadful gate,
Give us our star and our arrival.

In Regent's Park

These Sunday mornings Londoners delight –
　With or without the trotting child –
　　Their workday eyes grown mild
But with their panoply precise and spry,
The handsome pleasure-ways of parks to try.

Dahlias down the banks flow crisp and bright,
　The grass is winter-short and pungent,
　　Dipping oars are plangent,
And in the light mist, dripping grey like silk,
Water and trees and air seem smoothed in milk.

So that the forbidden island in the stream,
　The chimney that over Lords looms,
　　And those peculiar domes,
Might be near or distant illimitable miles;
And as the still sky breaks into a thousand gulls,

Might burst into some bright or strange kind,
  Or open into a different scale.
  To change in this style
Is the property, I find, of love, which brings
A new dimension to all physical things.

For if I see my park with Vivian's eye –
  The formal eye of a painter's mind –
  It is changed as under his hand,
And through the mists of his being are visible
Hints of glory before unimaginable.

One does not learn to look with another's eye
  For ever, but the rigid world
  Moves and is unfurled.
This is the effect and virtue of passion's part,
That trains the eye and exercises the heart.

Night Poem

Lord, our night is cursed with wings,
  Scolding conscience cries of war,
  Let not our time's cant veer
Us from godlike and private things,
  Where the world's shivering hulk despair –
  Like us – sustains.

If I wake to think his face
  Above me gazing a world distant,
  If he wake to think me pleasant
In his arms, let our embrace
  Hold no delusion, though an absent,
But the true grace:

Since we will not fool our minds
  To love any but the actual, nor
  Though this be what we were made for,
Think this love the world: its kind,
  Though it be our chief joy here,
  Is a lucky find.

But for him I may add my own prayer:
    Let me not be barren to him in his sleep,
    And that he his dreams may keep
Have both wolf and angel far;
    All he lose be his sins burnt up
In the night's fire.

On Two Photographs

With folded hands and pleasant grin,
    Indulgent to the unreal bird
Promised, my little love at nine
    Greets the camera with a reasonable word.

Years before, his baby eyes
    From gown of white and holy hill
Had faced the world, the camera's gaze,
    And hoped for good, but gravely feared for ill.

Childhood proved the hope not groundless,
    Set placid hands beneath the eyes
Still doubtful, and in free sweetness
    He grew toward the intended paradise.

When sensible, would run away;
    Found many things a source of pleasure;
Believed the half of what he saw;
    Played tricks, without repenting them at leisure.

Railways discarded, wished to film
    The life of Paul the missionary;
Till all these tastes were overwhelmed
    By love of paint, and of typography.

Light prints the matured image
    Now upon the world of Time:
This is mine; but old age
    I look after, and the sight will not come.

The essential face is turned to me,
But the expression cannot give
More than its gentleness, nor show
Which was truer, the hope or fear of grief.

A Letter

Lying in bed this morning, just a year
Since our first days, I was trying to assess –
Against my natural caution – by desire
And how the fact outdid it, my happiness:
And finding the awkwardness of keeping clear
Numberless flamingo thoughts and memories,
My dear and dearest husband, in this kind
Of rambling letter, I'll disburse my mind.

Technical problems have always given me trouble:
A child stiff at the fiddle, my ear had praise
And my intention only; so, as was natural,
Coming to verse, I hid my lack of ease
By writing only as I thought myself able,
Escaped the crash of the bold by salt originalities.
This is one reason for writing far from one's heart;
A better is, that one fears it may be hurt.

By an inadequate style one fears to cheapen
Glory, and that it may be blurred if seen
Through the eye's used centre, not the new margin.
It is the hardest thing with love to burn
And write it down, for what was the real passion
Left to its own words will seem trivial and thin.
We can in making love look face to face:
In poetry, crooked, and with no embrace.

Tolstoy's hero found in his newborn child
Only another aching, vulnerable part;
And it is true our first joy hundredfold
Increased our dangers, pricking in every street

In accidents and wars: yet this is healed
   Not by reason, but the endurance of delight
   Since our marriage, which, once thoroughly known,
   Is known for good, though in time it were gone.

You, hopeful baby with the erring toes,
   Grew, it seems to me, to a natural pleasure
In the elegant strict machine, from the abstruse
   Science of printing to the rich red and azure
It plays on hoardings, rusty industrial noise,
   All these could add to your inherited treasure:
      A poise which many wish for, writing the machine
      Poems of laboured praise, but few attain.

And loitered up your childhood to my arms.
   I would hold you there for ever, and know
Certainly now, that though the vacuum glooms,
   Quotidian dullness, in these beams don't die,
They're wrong who say that happiness never comes
   On earth, that has spread here its crystal sea.
      And since you, loiterer, did compose this wonder,
      Be with me still, and may God hold his thunder.

Kirkwall 1942

Far again, far,
And the Pentland howling psalms of separation
Lifts and falls, lifts and falls between.
But present pain
Folds like a firth round islets that contain
A sheepfold and a single habitation –
Moments in our summer of success –
Or the greater islands, colonized and built with peace.

Cold knives of light
Make every outline clear in a northern island,
The separating light, the sea's green;
Yet southern lives

Merge in the lupin fields or sleepy coves,
In crowstepped gables find a hint of Holland,
And Europe in the red religious stone:
All places in the room where we in love lie down.

Remember Him

Remember him when the wind speaks over a still bed
   In restless report; remember
   Him faring afar in danger –
Neutral stars and enemy sea – sped
By the will unwilling, steaming against the heart, against the blood,
   Faring for ever, and unimaginably far.

           And this is foolishness, for
           No parting is for ever,
        And all divergence meets in a round world.
           Yet it is now more vivid
           Than hope of ultimate good
        From this evil; while our dearest, filed
           Numbered inoculated comforted
           By a drug to dampen love, are forwarded
        To endure the life-giving sun, or to be killed.

Tropic of Cancer: yet even this we willed, though not foreseeing.
   It is now to remember
   The glory even there
   Where boredom, heartache and discomfort are.
Not in the News, where hills are plains and battles plain in
      meaning,
   The risk all past – but a senseless, timeless war.

        O all you lovers, listeners, when
        The strange sea flings him back again
        Into your arms, these histories hear
        Only as a wind that shakes the door
        And makes more grateful the good fire.
        I pray that comes: but now remember

Him in loneliness and danger,
And let the wind fill your ears,
For if imagination shares
His pain, he bears only
A divided burden, and a grief less lonely.

A Dream Observed

Out from his bed the breaking seas
    By waking eyes unseen
Now fall, aquatic creatures whirl
    And he whirls through the ambient green.

The sea lion and the scolopendra
    Lolling in sleep he sees
Strange in their ways, and the swift changes
    Their landscape makes, from shells to trees.

Down English lanes a camel walks,
    Or untrammelled flies.
But I, wakeful and watching, see
    How chilly out of the clothes he lies.

Easy an act to cover him warm:
    Such a lover's small success
Like the heaped mind so humble in sleep
    But points our actual powerlessness.

Monsters in dreams he sees, yet lies
    At peace in his curling bed;
Blessings that outdo all distress
    Implicit in his sleeping head.

A Mile from Eden

With buds embalmed alive in ice,
Flies in amber, the wood lies:
On snow even the shadows are white,
And we walk tipsy with too much light.
In slanting rays, like the damned
Our footsteps flame but make no sound.
While in this waste we wander
I tell him again of the godlike Flounder,
The garish desires of the fisherman's wife
(Desires we saw from the first unsafe,
For the same sin, though tropical,
Is in the Garden and the Fall).
But as I describe the granted glories,
The crowns, candles, golden floors,
I see his longing in his eyes:
Eyes of the humble hoping for Heaven,
Eyes of Adam a mile from Eden.
I see him a child with his joys round him,
One foot still on the coral strand,
The sun like a locket hung from his hand,
Now a man with his griefs about him.

If his hunger is holy, where hers was greed,
Can he always avoid the wish to be God?
Heaven revolves, distant, perfect,
Placid and impregnable as in a Collect;
And we walk in a waste of snows,
Yet see that power before our eyes
Which if we learn its usage can
Break up the amber, reverse the sun,
The bird's-eye glory to full sight
Bring, and outcasts into delight.

Before Sleep

Now that you lie
In London afar,
And may sleep longer
Though lonelier,
For I shall not wake you
With a nightmare –
Heaven plant such peace in us
As if no parting stretched between us.

The world revolves
And is evil;
God's image is
Wormeaten by the devil.
May the good angel
Have no rival
By our beds, and we lie curled
At the sound unmoving centre of the world.

In our good nights
When we were together,
We made, in that stillness
Where we loved each other,
A new being, of both
Yet above either.
So, when I cannot share your sleep,
Into this being, half yours, I creep.

Exile

To John

Exile you say is a sympathetic theme.
He that does but consider with compassion
All these extremes of sorrow and bloodshed
Must say it indeed. But consider only
The separations that harm, not kill:
Consider England exiled from Europe;
How many lack their lives' diurnal,

What houses are fallen, and what moments
Of perfection wrecked or denied.
How music struggles in a mausoleum
Where the ghosts of past sounds,
Unable to cease, confuse the living.
And remember that you and I
Have not exchanged a spoken syllable
Thirty months and more. Exile –
How should we do otherwise than harp upon exile,
While maps carry the departing lovers
In white and lengthening tracks; while
Daily we learn new names for fights
And farther off? Such a disease
Deceptively absorbs all others
(Or so I find): lack and longing,
Blocked roads and shortcomings,
Are all ascribed to this; this is
The dun cloud which hides the sun.

In a Dark Age, one thinks time and again
Of other such eclipses of light, and how it must have seemed then.
The vivid images of an inaccurate history crowd my mind,
But like the shapes of words, as they were when first learned
(Sound, sight, and the mouth that spoke), they lurk just behind me
And slip off as I turn.
Fifth-century England: a lamp in a cave where knowledge cowered;
Or I think of a grizzled old man, crying from an ivied tower
In the hushed insensate forest; of truth undigested
By the animal shapes that sheltered and kept it unmolested.
No one then, or at other times, expected a rebirth,
But in a breaking wave, in a bulrush cradle, it came unexpectedly,
And the darkness continued on earth.
Hard to separate darkness and light in one's own time so
        confidently,
Or, for me, to know whether I am really placed
Beside that solitary lamp, or out in the hulking forest.

                But you, no doubt of it, live at the centre,
                And with the sensations of darkness, work
                The effects of light, by bitter practice.
                Many might compass their own survival,
                In several generations acquiring a new sense.

This would be at best a cactus method,
Preservation, hardly creation.
But deprivation to the patient skilful
Is a means to make new.
This was a lesson you had by heart
Long ago, I suppose.
And long learnt in what respects
Writing may gain on speech: worked with
Wit and warmth, with scorn a sharp knife,
Time and space as a frame, forgotten
Like all good frames that point possession.
So are set cliffs and seas on a stage;
Over swamps, a road; on a flat canvas
Three dimensions. O little comfort
Comes to the maker, and when war ends
Still *we are exiles from our fathers' land*,
Exiles from heaven – pursue that no further.
For still the raw material of pain
Is changed into joy; for still a man
Acts above reasonable expectation;
Still the silence between men is broken;
And these are glories.

At Parting

Since we through war awhile must part
Sweetheart, and learn to lose
Daily use
Of all that satisfied our heart:
Lay up those secrets and those powers
Wherewith you pleased and cherished me these two years:

Now we must draw, as plants would,
On tubers stored in a better season,
Our honey and heaven;
Only our love can store such food.
Is this to make a god of absence?
A new-born monster to steal our sustenance?

We cannot quite cast out lack and pain.
Let him remain – what he may devour
We can well spare:
He never can tap this, the true vein.
I have no words to tell you what you were,
But when you are sad, think, Heaven could give no more.

For a Birthday

In a week will be your birthday:
And since it is a blessed day for us
I would not pass it unremembered.
Remembrance, but what wish? What
Should I send, over the damp Scotch miles
To where war keeps you, nailed to our farthest north,
To a stretched point in our mode of being,
Belonging by rights to the sleepy Arctic,
Warm and awake and ours by an accident?
A dark north
That yet glares with open eyes
All summer; an island that, however you tell me
Of cornfields, low cliffs, a paper-strewn shore,
Still is a rock for me,
Half hidden, steep in a snarling sea;
Still is the distant savage island
Of Lot's time, an island encrusted with names
Like barnacles – Morgause in a kind of shroud,
Lamorack murdered, Gawaine, Mordred,
Whose deeds and relationships, hard to remember,
Express our sin, our suffering, our self-knowledge.
Orkney: peat and storms; the overthrow of good –
And its resurrection, also hard to remember:
But that happened elsewhere.

And there, in an equally barbarous age
Again we send soldiers: but as we grow
Farther from the quick instinctive thrust
And battles are colder, always harder
Is the choice to go, more slow the transformation.

Hard, hard the return to childhood,
To obey the unexplained command,
With warmth and food a world's horizon.
The payday drunks, the friendly, the furious,
Neck by neck in a nissen hut.
Each may be a hero at any moment
Or an unwelcome bedfellow. There
You dwell, and are absent; impatient, yet at peace.

While I, in a happier position,
Yet maimed without you, cherish our child
(She being little, with no sense yet
Though much joy), dandle her with a double care
For her lack of you,
Mix together the scraps of the day
In letters for you,
Hoist sheaves in a high barn
And think of you;
Grub about at the roots of words,
Watch the land, go leasing, look little ahead.

Things being thus, what can I say?
I can certainly count considerable happiness,
Even good fortune, as ours: no ocean
Eats my words, though days delay them;
We live and are fed, our love is one will keep;
For us, words are a comfort, we partly command them;
We have a discipline and treasure in our child.
But years ago the glass was turned,
Glass ball with its image of a peaceful scene
Turned upside down, and the snowflake fugitives
Whirling, darkening the shape of Europe,
Blot out the lights and the village green.
Because of our parting, yes, but also
Because of those who endure far worse –
Jews and Gentiles, guilty or gentle,
Martyrs or mere sufferers – because of heartbreak
And the falling tower,
Falling now, and now rebuilt
By the future in the present, with perpetual tedious pain,
And because it seems in vain – dear as this day is,
I must wish you many returns, happier than this.

Bring Back

Salt sea, sweet sea,
Sail my lover back to me.

Then will winters lose their sting,
The dumb sorrow depart from spring;
I shall rise easy in the morning;
The endless afternoons will bring
No sick weariness to me;
I shall be beautiful and free.

I shall not hate the baby's crying –
I shall hear the turtle sing.
Taste shall equal scent; rejoicing
Really be now, not past or coming;
Having outdo desire, and longing
Lead to delight; all poetry
Emerge as it was meant to be.
And to be good will be easy.

If he returns across the sea
Shall all these mercies really be?

Shall we see raindrops upward rain,
Figs grow on thorn, and an end of pain,
Because your lover comes again?
Affluent hearts have power through
Their alembic to make life new –
But likelier life goes on as before.
Love can do all, but needs more
Than fortune and a rapturous hour.
Tedious and rare tasks are done
Ere rivers run dry and rocks melt with the sun.

Now as Then

September 1939

When under Edward or Henry the English armies
Whose battles are brocade to us and stiff in tapestries
On a green and curling sea set out for France,
The Holy Ghost moved the sails, the lance
Was hung with glory, and in all sincerity
    Poets cried 'God will grant to us the victory.'
For us, who by proxy inflicted gross oppression,
Among whom the humblest have some sins of omission,
War is not simple; in more or less degree
All are guilty, though some will suffer unjustly.
Can we say Mass to dedicate our bombs?
Yet those earlier English, for all their psalms,
Were marauders, had less provocation than we,
And the causes of war were as mixed and hard to see.
Yet since of two evils our victory would be the less,
And coming soon, leave some strength for peace,
Like Minot and the rest, groping we pray
    'Lord, turn us again, confer on us victory.'

Prayer in a Pestilent Time

Lord, for the year's apprehension,
    The soldier's dress, the civil pains,
And the expected cataclysm,
    Forgive, and deliver us from all our sins.

Now for the dread as darkness gathers,
    The lies like a gas that unseen burns,
For blindness, death and deprivation,
    Forgive, and deliver us from all our sins.

Deep our darkness, and powerless
    Our love: to Thee, darker the shroud
Of flesh and more reduced the glory,
    For us a boy, and a malefactor dead.

Deeper the darkness, the light greater.
    Bring us where such light remains.
After our knowledge, weariness and grief
    Forgive us all, and deliver us from our sins.

Ringshall Summer

Remembering Marvell's 'Appleton House'

Never was such a year for sun
At Ringshall as this dreadful one.
We seem sequestered on an island:
Bracken rolls for miles around,
The tips with silver sparkles shine,
And the green deeps close us in.
Though from that water come angry cries
Of soldiers at their practices,
Bobbing like boats in a rough sea
Above the fronds, in tank and lorry,
Or crouching camouflaged and slack,
Snails with their safety on their back;
And though the planes rove through our skies
Constantly, moving like jealous eyes
Over the house, and serve to warn
Us to expect the locust soon –
These only make our survival stranger,
Leaving us the unrivalled summer.

But while the shining of this sun
Making catastrophe seem unreal
Divides the mind, it joins in one
These outward forms. For I could call
The changing tide that laps the terrace
Where I work, water or flowers;
Roses roll right to our doors,
Whorls of white foam; snapdragon flares
Burn up in phosphorescent fires;
Pink and purple sweet-pea spools
Are coloured weeds in tropic pools.

The leaves part with flicker and leap
Of fish, where wrens court and creep
Stripping the grubs; when twilight comes
Our home a solitary lighthouse gleams,
And clumps of white daisies show
Where a shoal swims past the window.

Early, the air's thin silky blue
Only the finest sun lets through,
While through the wide-meshed air of evening
Pours the light of his coarsest shining.
In draughts the garden drinks it in.
Circus flowers of the haricot bean,
White waxy potato blooms, and green
Marrow, hidden in a flannel tent,
And curved like a wind instrument –
All are pleasant for what they promise,
Unlike flowers, grown for the eyes
To please at once, for when the frore
Weather has beaten our ships from shore,
Or hostile guns have bit too deep,
These shall defer the frozen sleep.

Even plants in the grass delight
The taste in fancy: yellow and white
In spring were milky curds here
Of cowslip and cuckoo flower;
Now eggs and bacon grow, and toad-flax
Hereabouts called buttered haystacks.
Mushrooms fatten in a night,
The yaffle sucking up ants takes fright,
And flies to the little spinney, that
A glacier under bluebells lay,
Rich and warm now with rose bay.
There he hangs, his body pressed
To the trunk, like a sailor on a mast:
Only his brilliant head betrays him,
Lolling back from the trunk which hides him.

Children, walking on a road, can say
They row in a boat, and thus they
Enjoy the double world, and know

The road both road and river; so
When I leave our hills for the plain below,
To cross the bracken I need a boat,
And from our porch with oars strike out.
When I was little, these fronds were tall
To make a tunnel or banqueting hall;
They still reach over my head, as pulling
Through their green waves gently rolling
I and my boat enter the grove
Out of the sunshine. As in a cove
That makes in monstrous cliffs a salient,
Each sound echoes, and makes more silent
The cove by contrast, and men speak soft,
Silence hangs in the trees. Aloft
A pigeon takes off with a sharp crack
Like a wave breaking against a rock.
Looking upwards I see no sky;
Delayed by leaves the light slips by
Mellow as honey. Here to look up
Is like gazing down through deep
Clear water, watching a pendent world
A touch will break; pale trunks rise whorled
With leaves like waving weeds, where
Birds quick as minnows cut the close air.

Below the woods widen the plains
As far as Oxford and the Thames,
And the church on its little hill of tombs
Floats over all: fields of barley
With prawn's whiskers, still white and creamy;
Wheat feathers brown or orange; oats
The first to be reaped, where lurk the rabbits
Close in the ever-lessening square
Uncut; they think, while they've an ear
Above their heads, life can go on,
Normal, though outside waits the gun.
Like us, they'd rather pretend than run.

This, then, is our summer country,
Wherein at times, remote and tiny,
I see my own familiar shape
Moving across a painted landscape.

But if the special character
Dividing forms can disappear,
Leaving the elements that they share;
And a human eye not only see
But cause this change, if it look rightly –
Jerusalem is not above all wars,
And wilder and more skilful eyes
Could see it now, and in these places.

For this Time

Now that the firmament on high,
Noah's peace-promising sky,
Is given over to an enemy,
And that those durable lights the stars
Fuse and explode, and friendly fires
Are travestied in the bomb's brightness,
And homes made hostile as the darkness;
Now country people look towards town,
And awestruck see the crimson stain
Spread on the cloud, and *London's burning*
Say in grief as once laughing:
From such a conflict, fire and frenzy,
Where should we turn unless Lord to Thee?
That Thou wouldst teach us to bear calmly
The invisible battles overhead,
And to get us through the night without dread.
Teach us therefore so to live
That we may fear our noisy bed
As little as our more peaceful grave.

Taliessin Reborn

'The ship and the song drove on'.   *Taliessin through Logres*.

I

At that time, some were disturbed by the music
Moving from the horizon,
But they were chiefly men who lived on the coast,
Who hearing could also see:
Saw that the moving music irritated the waters,
Saw waves flung and foam following,
While that country sea-coming
After the waves and the sound sailed slowly upon them:
Whose shores were birth, whose towers were order, whose
     woods in leafmeal the material of man.
Then in the bright and blinding mist of its approaching
It disappeared from sight.
Some were relieved and almost, though never quite, forgot;
But some were obliged to know that the being of this country
Through the passage of ear and eye had pierced into the heart,
And from that seat
Interpreted experience, taught them how
The time they breathed, earth they devoured, their rituals and
     their money,
The map too of seas and states, had here their form and relation.
But for the most part it came unheard,
Unseen, and was unsought.

II

But yet that country had long been visible
On clear days, to those that were capable,
From towers in the town, from hills and the sea-shore.
Some thought it a mirage and looked no more
(The flat vision of infancy not outgrown),
And some thought it – although as they would own
A fact in the landscape – not the soul's concern;
And there were some who could discern
The rock behind the mirage, through the spray
And rainbow of fancy the precise line; and few
Lastly the very few had seen
Cast on the level sand as if on a screen

Their own vast shadows: shapes of the true self
In the moment of heaven or the narrow eye of love –
The depth and height of an unguessed perfection –
But each split with a shaft of contradiction.
There was the real map of England: by
The deep valleys of potentiality
Rose the peaks of her fulfilled power;
The sprawling skerries of half-submerged desire
Confused the coasts, and the islands of plain longing.
A country of conscious being,
Of contemplated life. And some tried
To express in words the essence of what they descried.
They did not point the meaning – so indeed
The myth was to each according to his need:
This and his powers determined what he heard.
But after centuries the grooves grew blurred:
Myths of Arthur, the Grail, the Wounded King,
Were jumble for poets, play for children, a spring
Of endless ink for scholars, and still lacked full meaning.

III

So it was time that we saw it again,
And remembered that our footsteps echo in another world
(Even concrete cannot imprison that reverberation).
But now for our generation this world is understood,
Is named and commanded in its pathos and significance;
The symbols that would burn the naked hand
Conveyed to blood and heart by the insulation of verse.
This poetry of which I write, in its coarse flexible mesh,
Rich with a strange juxtaposition of colours,
Here and there snarled or gaudy, but still strong-fibred,
With common words in a strange dye, with knots of metaphysic –
This is the mesh that drew the loud myth so close
(The manuals coupled, the echo instantaneous),
This at last compelled the slow sea-coming
And loosed upon England the invisible virtues.

And now? Shall we know ourselves for what we might be,
Cease to fight, to rape the earth, to fear, cease even to die?
If any art could change us, or the strangeness of a myth,
We should have altered long ago. We remain as we were.

But like the Invisible Knight Garlon who punished unseen,
A terror, an outrage, yet finally a friend;
Like our seemingly wasteful and unforgivable pain,
And the insult of death – it is a holy ghost
That works among the fallen: nothing in the end is lost.

Now Philippa is Gone

Now Philippa is gone, that so divinely
Could strum and sing, and is rufus and gay,
Have we the heart to sing, or at midday
Dive under Trotton Bridge? We shall only
Doze in the yellow spikenard by the wood
And take our tea and melons in the shade.

Aisholt Revisited
For Olive Willis

These moors in August drank the burning sky,
And stretched out still thirsty, scorched by gorse,
Though the combes ran cool on either side
With waving fronds and streams to the red loam
And appeasing pasture. I have known them too
When birds and water and the young green seemed
One element: the holly like tracks of a snail
Glittered in the soft new larch, and the combes were brindled
With primroses; or later in full May
Have looked at midday down into a mineral fire
Of blue and green in the woods, and at dusk descended
Where rhododendrons held the shrunk light as glass does.
But ever Exmoor lay beautiful and hopelessly far,
With unknown turrets and the named points.
I have visited this place at different times
With those I love most, and each new visit
Found a fissure from the past, that may not be

Joined into the present, as in heaven,
And had, in the new pleasure, some sadness.
But I pray that the simplicity
And goodness of those days are not lost or corrupted;
As we in this country still remember Wordsworth,
At Alfoxton wonder how he could run the huge house,
And why he should start so late in the afternoon
On the walking tour that began the Ancient Mariner.
That was unaltered, though he grew old and stiff,
Though Coleridge was impossible to live with,
And Dorothy's brain grew soft by the fire.
The landscape was the occasion and the vessel.
So let our times beside the speaking streams,
In the secret cottage, or in the maze of combes,
By their intensity exist for ever.

The Cold Heart

Our Spring seems warm in his eyes and skin,
But his breath comes chilly – the heart must be of ice –
His blue runnels frigid and his crocus lazy.
And I have known anger at my heart like this,
When I did not desire it and I did not agree,
And the mind would have melted but the heart held hard.
But here on the hill, above noise and anger,
I am not in heaven, but have golden fields
Filmed into mauve where a cloud creeps over,
With a woof like tussore; the trees cough gently
Below by the yellow and magenta houses,
The black calf's visage is wreathed in smiles
As he humps to his feet, and high up the glider
Strays haphazard into shafts of light.
Sharp and green the paths downward leading,
Each the precipitation of the day's peace.

Zennor

For J.L. and L.B. Hammond

Seen from these cliffs the sea circles slowly.
    Ponderous and blue to-day, with waves furled,
    Slowly it crosses the curved world.
We wind in its waters with the tide,
    But the pendent ships afar
    Where the lightest blue and low clouds are
We lose as they hover and over the horizon slide.

When it was a dark blue heaven with foam like stars
    We saw it lean above us from the shore,
    And over the rocks the waves rear
Immense, and coming in with crests on fire;
    We could not understand,
    Watching the sea descend upon the land,
What kept it from flooding the world, being so much higher.

To-day it lies in place, and the dun houses,
    The apple-green cloudy oats, the cows that seem
    Compact of the yellow crust of their cream,
Shrink on Amalveor's grey and tawny sides,
    Sucking the last shreds of sun.
    But all life here is carried on
Against the crash and cry of the moving tides.

At Richmond

At Richmond the river is running for the city:
Though the tall houses on the hill and hotels
In white paint hint of the cliffs and broader sea,
He cannot falter nor alter from his nature.
Lord, neither let falsity my days dissipate.
I have been weak and injudicious in many things,
Have made my tongue an irritant against my intention,
Was calm only in convalescence after sin,
And have frequently feared. Then forgive
Yet once, bless and beckon to the broken city.

The Phoenix Answered

Sitting in this garden you cannot escape symbols,
  Take them how you will.
  Here on the lawn like an island where the wind is still,
    Circled by tides in the field and swirling trees,
    It is of love I muse,
Who designs the coloured fronds and heavy umbels,
    Second-hand marriage, not for passion but business,
    Brought on by the obliging bees.

This hedge is a cool perch for the brown turtle-dove,
  His phoenix unseen:
  Such was their love that perhaps they grew to be one.
    At first the mystical making one in marriage
    Had all my heart and my homage:
A fire and a fusion were what I wanted of love.
    But bodies are separate, and her fanatic bliss
    Left the phoenix bodiless.

Frosty burning cloud, delectable gate
  Of heaven hopelessly far,
  Though tilting almost to touch, whose holy fire
    Has no corrosive property unless
    Despair of it destroys us;
When in love, toward you our faces are set.
    Once I would win by the pains of passion alone,
    Aim at you still, that method outgrown.

If daily love now takes from these earlier ones
  The sweetness without the pain,
  The burning nights, the breathless fears gone,
    Peace in their place I never hoped to be given
    Unless if ever in heaven –
This is your own success, who have at once
    The unscathing fire and the ease of peace,
    All that I praise and bless.

Epithalamion

After a thousand possible perils –
A course kept, but at what cost of exhaustion,
What heartache, between frivolity and despair
(Those clashing rocks, oppositions joined for destruction)
Calmly to steer;
Moreover, to carry joy like a hurricane lamp,
All the way blazing delight on the dull and the doubtful –
After this, to come into lakes of peace,
Bright walks among oleanders by the waterside,
And mountains that do not creep unexpectedly close
Peering over one's shoulder, but hang translucent, distant.

That journey we know – all honour to you
Who made in the steep seas a passage through;
But the calm lake we must question a little.
No one now, ending a novel –
As they still end – at the steps of the altar,
Dares to assume it. 'Happily ever after'
Is not our cant: ours is different,
And *he flatters this age* whose bent
Is to call the *marmoset* an *ape*, the *swan* a *goose*,
All marriages unhappy, for this is our disease.
At a wedding, however, there are still bells,
Smiles, confetti, joy taken for granted.
Is this a superstition, decayed but undaunted?
Of this I am certain: there will be joy
For you, of the kind that no sorrow can destroy.
And yet by many it is not seen as such:
Not because they expect too much
(For in love we grasp more than we thought to reach,
By God's grace), but because they subject it
To the wrong tests, and lose while they dissect it.
Expecting, too, to be perpetually aware
Of happiness, when the full consciousness is rare:
For it is our common and strange condition
Not to know what we are, nor when we are in heaven.
Marriage may take us thither; but if we look either
For complete union with the being of another,
Or for the separate fulfilment of the self,
We see neither: the texture of love

Is of both, indivisible; something is made
By lovers which neither singly could.
A complex result, and as hard to define
(Though with singular ecstasy known)
And to the eye as little apparent
As the effect of an electrical current.
The inert metal is active, changed
By a borrowed force, and the two are merged;
Yet the life is its own, with which it is charged.
And then, so they say, nothing ought to look the same.
As to that, I remember from my childhood a game,
Half fear, half delight. We shut our eyes,
Then, opening them, found the identical place,
The identical grown-ups, drowsy in their chairs,
But we had travelled far, and were strangers.
If we spoke to them, they did not understand,
The familiar drawing-room was in a foreign land
And we had never met. I could not decide
How much truth there might be in what they said,
And was half disappointed, half relieved when
The game was over and they knew us again.

Thus I think that even though
Things look as usual, you will know
A difference, hardly to be taken for peace,
That will be so, none the less.
This at times both body and soul
Feel, and find themselves made whole
Before they knew it, or knew their need.
O, if the joy were not so deep
Who would bear children, or have faith
So to prefer life before death?

But you, dear and delightful, known
And loved so long, possess your own
Perfection, with a gaiety,
A brilliance which I have quite passed by
In this long tortuous meditation
Meant for your marriage. Jubilation
Flames upon your forehead still
And warms me, as when we emerged from school,
With bursting hearts, inquisitive eyes,

Perplexed at evil, dazzled with joys,
To travel wrapped in our own concerns,
And see great cities on our own terms;
Our growing-pains compressed within
The marvellous walls of a violin.

Our past should stay in the past: I name it
Only to invoke a blessing from it.
By the round castle and the roofs of Rome;
By the stuffy cardboard music-room;
By the Scotchmen red and black
At dawn in distant farms; Will's Neck
And burning moor; Saint Francis' hill;
By the pillars of the ruined concert-hall –
I bless you; by the incalculable powers
Of music, the many and hard hours
Of work that make one excellence –
In a single act of benevolence
I would join these, as best I may,
For both, and for your wedding day.
Still I have said but a small part.
I wish you heaven with all my heart.

For Robin and Kirstie

Again earth enters the cold tunnel,
    Warm beams barely burnish the air
Icy and as crisp as silk;
    Only the trees are left on fire:
    And we have lasted a year of war.

The summer that brought disaster and death
    Still brought you safely from the island,
Left us our lives and the knowledge of love.
    The year is not wholly unkind
    Whose tide-fall leaves such treasure behind.

Now raiders whistle the wind
   Wherever it blows, and make the distance
Wider between your hills and ours:
   Yet still the fact of your existence
   Is comfort and is confidence.

For I remember the delight I had –
   And may have – in your company:
In many mundane and cheerful things,
   But in music chiefly,
   That is both human and heavenly.

Soon we may learn to fear our beds
   As little as our quieter graves:
Meanwhile I send to you, dear cousins,
   Thanks and a blessing for your lives,
   And pray God to preserve your loves.

The Startling Answer

The knowledge that fear, though absent, will return
   Late or soon,
The likeliness of bereavement, the certainty of death,
   The insatiable demands of faith –
These in peace; then add the bludgeoning of war,
And still remains (apart from actual despair)
   The unreasoning expectation
Of natural joy some time, in some condition.
   Happiness we take as a right,
   The first fingers of light
Press hope under our morning lids, and bright
Colours in a baby's patchwork quilt control
Dark squares of the future, hope is the key of the whole.
Extraordinary labour is expended
In plans for a new world, when the bad times are ended.

But if it were all taken?
The adored lover in whom even self-love is forgotten,
    The toddler stilled and the roof-tree rotten,
The land that took the impress of the heart
Flattened; the heart itself bruised at the root:
    All gone, no hopeful chance any more
    In the opening of a door,
The hand on a letter; nothing new to be tried
After the poplar's whisper in the dark outside,
So that a new world offered no interest or return,
    What should we do then?
Some, so tough is the quality of man,
    Making of hopeless love
A plain dry daylight, would work on unmoved:
Work for what can never be achieved
    And must be willed.
But hope is yet their answer, altered, but still
The imperishable substance in a glass retort.

Lord, save us from the need of such a heart.
The humbler poise is hard enough to get:
    Convert us, but not yet.

Geordie

> *Geordie shall be hung in chains of gold*
> *So fine there never were any;*
> *For Geordie came of the royal blood*
> *And he courted a royal lady.*

> ---

> *And by that bed there standeth a stone . . .*

I came in May through an English country
    Where the green is richer than gold
And the brocaded gardens cool and dazzling,
    Until I reached a certain field.

There was a hill, and on the hill a gallows
Where Geordie hung in gold chains;
The girl beneath, in the sick scent of may,
Could not avert or share his pains.

A princess – and the chains in sunlight shone,
Uselessly bright and fine as fire.
Then I said to her: 'Why had Geordie to die
With all your hopes, a death so unfair?

What possessed him to steal the white deer,
Knowing the penalty – something he did not need?
The seed is not smaller in regard to the tree
Than this act to Geordie, who hangs dead.'

She answered: 'There is nothing can join
Such an effect to any cause.
O this death that bereft me of my beauty
Is constrained to its own laws.

The stealing – that was a trivial irrelevant act,
That was nothing to him or to me.
Some obstinacy forced the act on the thought:
Not that, nor even the judge, set up this tree.'

'Lady, what was this man more than another,
Or will you marry another man?'
'Geordie had wits, beauty, certainly had skill:
These are not the cause I can love him alone.

There is none to be defined or found, as none for his death.
And if Geordie had gentleness, wealth,
Gold was no good to him, nor did birth avail him,
Kindness could not keep him in health.

All his birth gained was to be hung in gold:
The judge turned round and promised me this.
I came here with arms to fight for his rescue,
But gained only his arms and a kiss.

What is the use to fight or blame for those
Whom unexplained the falcon tears?
Since *Corpus Christi* was written on the stone
He must accept both consequence and cause.'

For B.M.

who died by an accident in childhood

If the same world, its dayspring gone,
Runs upright in its grooves, day after day,
Who would believe it, till his own
Experience taught him? Yet he then
Must learn the bitter new exercise of joy,
He must drink death and master his happiness again.

These matters are too hard for me.
Only I know that looking direct at heaven
All is a blur of tears, but we
Searching our world's dark disc to see
What light or hope are there, may yet be given
A sight of perfection through the keener edge of the eye.

Loss is a dark sky; death a darkness.
But slanting from this depth, our eyes perceive
Shape in a short life's completeness.
Greater years might add new graces,
But not by changing this: new facets give
In crystal, new reflections of the original brightness.

A good world nurtured this boy:
The pilgrim's hill and immense distances of childhood;
Above him the balloons of joy and joke,
Who seemed to sing even when he spoke,
Calling on shawls and favourite things, who could
Hear in the ear's long shell the seas of music cry.

That shell cries perpetual peace
Now, and bright for ever is the holy hill.
That is for him; and if our eyes
Have bright margins, it must suffice.
May the dark central cone diminish, till
Above the disc of eye and earth the full glory rise.

For a Child Expected

Lovers whose lifted hands are candles in winter,
Whose gentle ways like streams in the easy summer,
Lying together
For secret setting of a child, love what they do,
Thinking they make that candle immortal, those streams forever
    flow,
And yet do better than they know.

So the first flutter of a baby felt in the womb,
Its little signal and promise of riches to come,
Is taken in its father's name;
Its life is the body of his love, like his caress,
First delicate and strange, that daily use
Makes dearer and priceless.

Our baby was to be the living sign of our joy,
Restore to each the other's lost infancy;
To a painter's pillaging eye
Poet's coiled hearing, add the heart we might earn
By the help of love; all that our passion would yield
We put to planning our child.

The world flowed in; whatever we liked we took:
For its hair, the gold curls of the November oak
We saw on our walk;
Snowberries that make a Milky Way in the wood
For its tender hands; calm screen of the frozen flood
For our care of its childhood.

But the birth of a child is an uncontrollable glory;
Cat's cradle of hopes will hold no living baby,
Long though it lay quietly.
And when our baby stirs and struggles to be born
It compels humility: what we began
Is now its own.

For *as the sun that shines through glass*
So Jesus in His Mother was.
Therefore every human creature,
Since it shares in His nature,
In candle-gold passion or white

Sharp star should show its own way of light.
May no parental dread or dream
Darken our darling's early beam:
May she grow to her right powers
Unperturbed by passion of ours.

For a Christening
Meditation and Invocation

I

In June the early signs,
And after, the steady labour of subcutaneous growth:
Past the danger of dissolution in the third month,
And in the fifth, quickens.
But hidden while the leaves thicken, through the season when
    smooth corn
Grows bearded, through the peeling of the summer's gold fleece;
Hidden but with heart throbbing, while stars sharpen and throb
    in the skies,
While sunsets grow cold and orange, while winter airs are
    whirled and torn;
And at Candlemas with pain is born.
Lying with a right occipital position, what prompts it we may
    never know,
But at the appointed time dives down, down into the light –
Blinding snow-light, piercing the darkest corner with white,
Brightness of prick-eared cyclamen pink against the snow –
So long hidden, so sudden into sight.

II

You are our darling and our foreign guest;
We know all your origins, and this is to know nothing.
Distinguished stranger to whom we offer food and rest;
Yet made of our own natures; yet looked for with such longing.
Helpless wandering hands, the miniature of mine,
Fine skin and furious look and little raging voice –
Your looks are full human, your qualities all hidden:
It is your mere existence we have by heart, and rejoice.
The wide waters of wonder and comprehension pour

Through this narrow weir, and irresistible their power.
The rainbow multiple glory of our humanity cannot pierce
As does the single white beam of your being.
This makes your presence so shattering a grace,
Unsheathed suddenly from the womb: it was none of our intending
To set in train a miracle; and yet it is merely
Made palpable in you, missed elsewhere by diffusion.
Therefore we adore God-in-our-flesh as a baby:
Whose Being is His Essence, and outside It, illusion.
Later, the fulfilment, the example, death, misprision –
Here the extraordinary fact of Being, which we see
Stripped and simple as the speechless stranger on my knee.

III

Blessing, sleep and grow taller in sleeping.
Lie ever in kind keeping.
Infants curl in a cowrie of peace
And should lie lazy. After this ease,
When the soul out of its safe shell goes,
Stretched as you stretch those knees and toes,
What should I wish you? Intelligence first,
In a credulous age by instruction cursed.
Take from us both what immunity
We have from the germ of the printed lie.
Your father's calm temper I wish you, and
The shaping power of his confident hand.
Much, too, that is different and your own;
And may we learn to leave you alone.
For your part, forgive us the pain of living,
Grow in that harsh sun great-hearted and loving.
Sleep, little honey, then; sleep while the powers
Of the Nine Bright Shiners[1] and the Seven Stars
Harmless, encircle: the natural world
Lifegiving, neutral, unless despoiled
By our greed or scorn. And wherever you sleep –
My arms outgrown – or waking weep,
Life is your lot: you lie in God's hand,
In His terrible mercy, world without end.

[1] See 'Green Grow the Rashes O', *English County Songs*, ed. Lucy Broadwood,
where a note explains that in one English interpretation, as in the Hebrew version,
it refers to the nine months preceding birth.

The Glance

Strange eyes for a baby,
And disconcerting. They ought not yet to express
Any perplexity, we think: still less
A flash of fear in trust.
Hard to bear such a tremulous look. Did
You just detect that a parent is not a god?

Any glance could tell
The whole truth, for here the body still
Speaks for the soul and has no separate will.
Kindled in joy, cursive in form like those
Baroque babies that float in Venetian skies,
You express a plain fact in an elaborate pose.

Wildness of gesture, the round
Calm shape of a cloud, precision of a kitten, are found
In one fat baby, with much that can never be learned
From any painted boy:
The riches in a chuckle, the rays of joy,
The changing moons of light in a living eye.

Yet much is already hidden:
Secret stir of the brain, secret ways
To turn my will, and test my strength of purpose.
And then, what possible relation
Exists between the darling of one moment
And the crimson barbarous brat of another instant?

Relation is seen in the whole.
The rage that from the first corrodes the soul
Even for a tiny child is pain to feel.
Aware but unreflective,
It dreads in me the force of its future anger,
Trusts in love, and will know it to be the stronger.

Christmas and Common Birth

Christmas declares the glory of the flesh:
And therefore a European might wish
To celebrate it not at midwinter but in spring,
When physical life is strong,
When the consent to live is forced even on the young,
Juice is in the soil, the leaf, the vein,
Sugar flows to movement in limbs and brain.
Also, before a birth, nourishing the child,
We turn again to the earth
With unusual longing – to what is rich, wild,
Substantial: scents that have been stored and strengthened
In apple lofts, the underwash of woods, and in barns;
Drawn through the lengthened root; pungent in cones
(While the fir wood stands waiting; the beech wood aspiring,
Each in a different silence), and breaking out in spring
With scent sight sound indivisible in song.

Yet if you think again
It is good that Christmas comes at the dark dream of the year
That might wish to sleep ever.
For birth is awaking, birth is effort and pain;
And now at midwinter are the hints, inklings
(Sodden primrose, honeysuckle greening)
That sleep must be broken.
To bear new life or learn to live is an exacting joy:
The whole self must waken; you cannot predict the way
It will happen, or master the responses beforehand.
For any birth makes an inconvenient demand;
Like all holy things
It is frequently a nuisance, and its needs never end;
Strange freedom it brings: we should welcome release
From its long merciless rehearsal of peace.

So Christ comes
At the iron senseless time, comes
To force the glory into frozen veins:
His warmth wakes
Green life glazed in the pool, wakes
All calm and crystal trance with living pains.

And each year
In seasonal growth is good – year
That lacking love is a stale story at best;
By God's birth
All common birth is holy; birth
Is all at Christmas time and wholly blest.

Aquarius, Aries

My Candlemas first-born, cherry in a field of frost;
My second, copper and gold in an Easter garden –
Plum blossom and the bicker of children's voices,
Almond blossom dropped on a silver quilt –
Such their nativities, their cradle images.
Beyond the pane, red poplar fences the sky:
The leaves are new-born. Image of a green tree,
Stared at long enough, enters the room, the eye
Plants green along the bedroom wall, as a saint
Long gazing at God, sees only Him – not
Precise in form, but a colour, a presence everywhere.
So I am haunted by this dialectic of birth
That colours every concept. Double face
Of love in a new countenance, a single;
The new life – changing love unchanged only
As a counterpoint of triple with duple time –
Is a child, fresh, fragile-seeming, yet tough.

Dreadful that this is a matter of our choice
To make or to withhold, a man have power
To offer immortality through his pleasure.
Yet only the refraining is wholly known –
The act, in darkness, and the sequel, hidden.
Even the birth, activity so intense,
Must be awaited passively, the pain
Must be endured – yet we are free to quicken it,
Or to hinder if we merely endure.

After a birth, that is the time for peace:
The wild creating will awhile appeased
As with no other creation – that is the time
To be still, time to rest and receive joy.
No reason yet to feel remorse, no pain
Yet to have been the instrument of pain,
Able as yet to satisfy and comfort,
Able to answer all with milk and stillness.
Later, must helpless watch the waste and sadness
While this small being strives to the second perfection.
Gift of life, not to be finally forgiven
Except in heaven: prerogative of God
Used without God's foreknowledge or compassion.
Is it our fault? When you were born you cried,
April and winter babes alike, but later
Chuckled and drank the light, inherited words
Concise and round as buds, and morning joys.
Yet for this you must grow to be ungrateful,
We must lose you, learn to rejoice in the loss.
A mutual pardon then, a mutual blessing,
For multiple love and the strange benefit of birth.
Aquarius, Aries, patterns of winter and spring –
O little children, may the signs favour your setting forth.

Crab Apple and the Crab's Tropic

Over the lucid Maytime sky
Falls the shadow of the Ice Saints going by.

We shiver, and the easterly wind
With crabbed fingers, following them close behind

Shrivels the frigid bluebells, chills
The blossom of the crab tree into icy frills.

Nothing on earth seems so cold
As springtime flowers suddenly out of season and old.

The Saints' shadow hints that Death
Is implied in the warm and first as well as the last breath.

And the child we began together –
A world ago it seems, in last year's summer weather –

Is born, and you not with me,
And still there is no word from you across the sea.

You in the Crab's tropic need
No reminding that we move close to the dead;

But there his claws are fire, not ice,
And the mantis' praying pincers mimic the saint's guise.

The humid fertile jungle mocks
Human fertility and warmth. Poison lurks

In the cool creek, in the sticky white
Snake-envelopes; the very flowers have fangs to bite;

And the loved sun is an enemy.
These worlds too far apart to share except in fancy:

But with an effort of faith we pass
Where the sun and snowy crab are temperate, equal the glass –

The common climate of our love.
Here we share the child's outsetting, deathless live and move.

Sketches

AUTUMN DAY

The raging colour of this cold Friday
Eats up our patience like a fire,
Consumes our willingness to endure.
Here the crumpled maple, a gold fabric,
The beech by beams empurpled, the holy sycamore,
Berries red-hot, the rose's core –
The sun emboldens to burn in porphyry and amber.

Pick up the remnants of our resignation
Where we left them, and bring our loving passion,
Before the mist from the dark sea at our feet
Where mushrooms cling like limpets in the grass,
Quenching our fierceness, leaves us in a worse case.

WINTER DAY

The shallowing purple beams, the sallow skies,
Blue airs and tides of light that wash above snows –
Snow whose images were yesterday all of eating:
White luscious globes in the wood, cocoanut icing
Outside in the crisping sun; chopped and broken
Into chocolate flake with the brown bracken –
All gone to-day in the blizzard, as when you turn
The crystal over, and break the rigid scene
Into a toy storm. We in the world's whirling
Sit poised in a lantern, skies all breaking
Hurling around us, time disintegrating
Where instants melt like snow. Yet we are whole –
He is here for a few days more; within this wall
Is lightness, quiet: tough and transparent flies
Our happiness in the swinging falling skies.

THE CRANES

We thought they were gulls at first, while they were distant –
The two cranes flying out of a normal morning.
They circled twice about our house and sank,
Their long legs drooping, down over the wood.
We saw their wings flash white, frayed at the black tip,
And heard their harsh cry, like a rusty screw.
Down in the next field, shy and angular,
They darted their long necks in the grass for fish.
They would not have us close, but shambled coyly,
Ridiculous, caught on the ground. Yet our fields
Under their feet became a fen; the sky
That was blue July became watery November,
And echoing with the cries of foreign birds.

Bathing in the Windrush

Their lifted arms disturb the pearl
And hazel stream
And move like swanbeams through the yielding
Pool above the water's whirl
As water swirls and falls through the torn field.

Earth bears its bodies as a burden:
Arms on a bright
Surface are from their shadows parted,
Not as the stream transforms these children
But as time divides the echo from the start.

Smiling above the water's brim
The daylight creatures
Trail their moonshine limbs below;
That melt and waver as they swim
And yet are treasures more possessed than shadows.

This wonder is only submarine:
Drawn to the light
Marble is stone and moons are eyes.
These are like symbols, where half-seen
The meaning swims, and drawn to the surface, dies.

Beads from Blackpool

In that town, nothing is sane but the sea.
Thank God, the waves break all winter over the
Ice-cream caves and fairy grottoes, over the
Lavatory bricks, the scaffolds of flimsy fun,
Ring contempt through rungs of the pier, fling
Black spray among the crowds, orphaned of summer,
Who nose the shops and gaze at boards announcing
Epstein's *Jacob*, erotic displays, and oysters.
Thank God the sea is ruthless.
They might have thought to teach this lesson, who chose
Blackpool for Overseas Assembly – showing

The ugliness men love, the wisdom of divorce.
But we refused it, briefly met to part
In a curtainless room converted from a shop,
Parting in agony behind the plateglass window.
It went hard with us, went hard with others
More silent than we, more used to obey
In silent rebellion.
                              Was there good in this?
I make no judgement yet, nor judge for the rest;
The time is dark yet, I am yet uncertain
If I accept that parting.

After bodily death, is death rejected
By the still-living self – through all advance
Felt still as an outrage, only in glory
Alas only in glory to be understood?
Life in our hands, we grope again to each other.
By what sensible link? Amber beads
Bought in the shamming town – Beads from Blackpool
(The fiery kind, solid wine, or flame
Bound in the stone against all inward change,
Docile to change of light and to our possession).
Now the child, immanent then, well born
Now and six months old,
Sucks, and while I nourish her and cherish her,
Seizes the beads with vague violent fingers.
So men clutch at hope. The seas break
And fade, the parting is past and still unsolved,
The miles shudder between,
And the obstinate flame, lovelocked in a living palm,
Speaks of sequence, denies the absolute death.

Still Life

Night fell and the fog froze;
Six-pointed Venus first and then the moon rose.
Preparing granite against the morning
Fog was petrified; the moon shone, wailing.
The moon's light is visible silence:

In her quietness all is quiet, in suspense
Between the day and darkness a dubious[1] brilliance
Every movement seems (unfocused) stealthy;
Rabbit across the lawn, stoat in the spinney,
On furtive errands. And within that light
There seems a presence waiting, just out of sight,
Holding its breath, waiting, the whole night.

Sleep, wake, sleep: it is there, just out of sight.

Night passed and the fog froze;
The moon passed, but not her silence: when the sun rose,
Rigid and mute his world, a fist
Clenched and contracted, every branch and plant encased
In quartz and scored with siliceous white –
A world struck solid and paralysed with light.

Absolute calm, absolute silence
Both to the eye and ear, but the skin feels violence,
Feels a pain whose origin is lost –
Impotent burning of the sun, or grip of the deaf-mute frost.

[1] *Dubious*: recalling its derivation from *duo*, two, as in *twi*light.

Dead and Gone

1

'O that it were possible we might
But hold some two dayes conference with the dead'
                    Duchess of Malfi

The coffin's typical shape
Implies for each a dear particular form:
The glory that was loved, caressed, endured,
Is carrion now, concealment but betrays it;
Hidden but known, lifeless but still the precious being.
Therefore, though each in pain is wholly alone,
The coffin is a common painful secret
Making of each an unwilling schizophrene:

For, what the imagination dares, the heart
Refuses; what the eye perceives, the heart
Knows to be falsehood; what the heart cries out
Receives an absolute negative from reason.

Then were all the other meetings traitors?
All those journeys when we flew and shone
Because toward each other, went toward this?
The perpetual hope, the hidden part of symbols,
Meant simply this: a sudden, public, death?
The dead could tell, but shares our longings no longer;
For once unfriendly, knows the whole or nothing
And shares nothing.
                                        Yet we cannot part.
Till we confront his life with this his death
And make one sense of both, all thought's uncertain
All memory unsolved, and our condition
Changes from apathy to agony, either
Equally profitless.

2

'For in the resurrection they neither marry, nor are
given in marriage'
                            St Matthew's Gospel

The specialty of time and place
Were of love's making, and are gone;
From the unfocused blur of space
And the indifference of time
Struck by the force of joy or pain –
These will never come again.

True, the environment retains
A faithful passion: earth or stone,
Archway, tree or moving-stair –
The place cries out, cries out in pain:
Its cries are heard by you alone,
The moment will not come again.

So place is widowed. What remains?
Sayings and anniversaries,
Saints'-days that loss discovers,

Hagiography of lovers;
Worst, the gradual death of pain,
For the image will not come again.

And after such a loss, what gain?
Not the longed-for, that is certain.
Nothing, or else a new thing.
If there is any final meeting
It is past desire or pain.
If love is, love is to be born again.

3

'He is dead and gone, Lady'
        Song

But O these dead, in dreams, in dreams returning.
So nearly true, they make awaking grief,
So far from true, that the true pain is relief.
Cruel, fickle, dissatisfied, sad,
Their life-like, life-betraying forms
Disquiet the night, disquiet the grave.
For it is we who haunt the dead
And not the dead haunt us – even
We tempt them, if their love constrains them
Still to will what we desire.

In dreams, in dreams returning. So we pursue them
With phantoms from a common past
Unexorcised. But lay these ghosts at last.
Why should Felicity long for us? Why should we wish it?
If death is double-faced, and turns
An opening look towards another world
That's out of sight. For present acquaintance, this:
The lids closed with cold coins,
The lips ajar, not for love
(This is neither enemy nor friend),
And yet for love to recognize the end.

Edlesborough

Beyond the Chiltern coast, this church:
A lighthouse in dry seas of standing corn.
Bees hive in the tower; the outer stone
Pared and frittered in sunlight, flakes with the years:
Clunch crumbles, but silence, exaltation endures.

The brass-robed Rector stretched on his tomb endures.
Within, we go upon the dragon and the bat,
Walk above the world, without,
Uplifted among lavender, beech and sycamore,
Shades of the sea-born chalk, indelible and austere.

If we see history from this hill
It is upon its own conditions, here
Each season swirls and eddies the circle of a year
Round the spectator church, and human eyes
Take, on its plinth, a long focus of centuries.

We seem like gods on any hill.
From here all toil resembles rest, and yet
Unlike a god we feel ourselves shut out.
Surely that farm in a carved blue curve of trees,
So still with all its creatures, holds the unattainable peace?

It is Time's camouflage deceives us.
There it extends like space: whatever moves
(A horse to drink, a reaper to stack the sheaves)
Displays the movement in its whole succession,
Not a change of terms, only a changed relation.

Deceit or truth? The dead possess the hill
In battlements of totternhoe or slate;
The view is ours, the range and ache of sight.
Their death, our life, so far apart, unite
If Time serves: in a common space unrolls
This Resurrection field, with sheaves in glory like risen souls.

Expectans Expectavi

The candid freezing season again:
Candle and cracker, needles of fir and frost;
Carols that through the night air pass, piercing
The glassy husk of heart and heaven;
Children's faces white in the pane, bright in the tree-light.

And the waiting season again,
That begs a crust and suffers joy vicariously:
In bodily starvation now, in the spirit's exile always.
O might the hilarious reign of love begin, let in
Like carols from the cold
The lost who crowd the pane, numb outcasts into welcome.

For a Christmas Broadcast: I

WOMAN'S VOICE

Perhaps you find the angel most improbable?
It spoke to men asleep, their minds ajar
For once to admit the entrance of a stranger.
Few have heard voices, but all have made a journey:
The mind moves, desiring dedication,
Desiring to lay its gifts, as a dog its bone,
At the feet of the first creation. 'Take it or leave it,'
Says pride, 'You made it; You must bear the blame.'
But secretly the heart – 'O make it good!
Either God acts in vain, or this is God.'

FIRST KING

Melchior brings gold. O teach me to give,
For this was infancy's first love:
Its first possession; its adult passion –
    O new creation
Take my treasure, so make me free.

SECOND KING

Caspar, incense: all that is strange,
Oblique, projected beyond the range
Of the First Person. Such mediation
    O new creation
Take, that we dare the direct sight.

THIRD KING

Death is a strong wish, Balthasar
Brings his desire in a gift of myrrh;
Seeking perfection in pain and cessation –
    O new creation
Die for me, make me desire to live.

ALL THREE

Mary, who nourished glory on human kindness
By springs of power hidden from the mind,
Here is our small self-knowledge, now
Make it acceptable, or teach us how.

MARY

    He will accept it, never fear,
    For his audacity is my despair.
    O do not give what he should not bear.
    His boldness is beyond belief,
    His threats, his lightnings, his short grief.
    Is it divine or mortal confidence?
    Mortal ignorance, godlike innocence.
    Brazen, he takes love as a right;
    He knows to demand is to give delight.
    Youngling, here we offer love;
    What have we to offer but love?
    And what is our love? Greed and despair,
    O do not take what you should not bear.
    Or tainted love by true convince:
    Let us not harm you, helpless Prince.
    Sin is the chance of mercy;
Then even sin contrives your greater glory.

For a Christmas Broadcast: II

(Carol: 'This have I done for my True Love.' *The first
stanza and refrain sound as if from behind closed doors.*)

FIRST KING

Behind this door, what shall we find?

SECOND KING

Reasonable men, though we came in a wild season:
We did not listen to angel songs on a hillside,
Nor birds with guttural messages from the gods.
These cold nights, too easy to imagine prophecies,
With the glittering heavens splitting through the brain;
We did not dream, we moved along the beam of logic.

THIRD KING

Reason moved us, in this bitter season,
Over the crumping snows, with all above
The seedling stars cast about the sky.

FIRST KING

Stars are spirits, Fravashi: this young one had
A new movement in the sidereal dance.

SECOND KING

Behind this door lies its human part.

FIRST KING

Behind this door, what Prince or Saint?

SECOND KING

                                  Or horror?
That strange song, and the dirty barbarous place –
Some god with an ass's head?

THIRD KING

                               Do not open,
Not yet, wait a little.

FIRST KING

We must open,
Or else time is lost for ever. Open.

(second stanza of carol bursts out)

SECOND KING

O powerless Glory
Forgive me. Bless me.
This is a mystery
Far too hard for me.
That Splendour should lie
On a woman's knee,
Clamorous, urgent,
Yet still innocent;
Burn like the stars
In a cold barn,
With the clanging spheres,
The sword-notes of pain,
The beasts' talking,
The angels' loud crying –
I am afraid.
Where is the stillness
The expected peace?
In all this violence
Where is the silence?

FIRST KING

There, in the dance.

THIRD KING

You are a marvel
And we – are here;
Nowhere else but here,
This our only claim.
Our gifts were precious
But now we find them
Only the specious
Love of our own natures:
Our making, our rituals
And our death.

These are all we have:
Take from your creatures
Their poor self-love.

FIRST KING

You are a marvel
And all is well.
O Love enliven us,
O gentle Chance
Not too late enlighten us
Call us to your dance.

(*Refrain:* 'Sing O my Love, O my Love, my Love, my Love,
This have I done for my true Love.')

The Spring Equinox

Now is the pause between asleep and awake:
Two seasons take
A colour and quality each from each as yet.
The new stage-set
(Spandrel, column and fan) of spring is raised against the winter
    backdrop
Murrey and soft;
Now aloft
The sun swings on the equinoctial line.
Few flowers yet shine:
The hellebore hangs a clear green bell and opulent leaves above
    dark mould;
The light is cold
In arum leaves, and a primrose flickers
Here and there; the first cool bird-song flickers in the thicket.
Clouds are pale as the pollen from sallows;
March fallows are white with lime like frost.

This is the pause between asleep and awake:
The pause of contemplation and of peace,
Before the earth must teem and the heart ache.
This is the child's pause, before it sees

The choice of one way has denied the other;
Must choose the either or both, of to care and not to care;
Before the light or darkness shall discover
Irreparable loss; before it must take
Blame for the creature caught in the necessary snare;
Receiving a profit, before it holds a share.

The Autumn Equinox

For my parents, at their Golden Wedding

The rose, whose shape's most perfect before its prime,
Contains at every stage a kind of perfection:
When the corolla is blown, the heart remains,
The flaming heart, so stored with the flower's life
That whoso eats of it devours the essence,
And takes all seasons of the rose for food.
And thus the beauty blown can nourish birds and men.

The autumn pause between awake and asleep
When night and day are equal, has this quality,
Hints of every season: the spring's hope
Which is its pain; the lazy power of summer;
Even the winter's ascetic suspense of power,
With a pinch of frost, and old-man's-beard on hedgerows
Dingy snow – all contrive an instant's contemplation.

Senescence which the soul rejects is alien –
The canker on the rose, the cell's rebellion.
Those are lucky and rare in whom it seems
The rose's heart, the autumn's equal season.
They make their past a nourishment for men;
After a long love know so true a wedding
That what the green desired, the golden finds fulfilled.

The Same Process

The cloud of winter wears away
And the bowed rosemary, under its death of snow
Keeps the everlasting green,
Whether for birth or burial, keeps the keen
And earth-fresh scent beneath the sterile weight;
While indoors the sick scent of mortal illness
Hangs like patience in the stillness
Under the roof where Death grows great,
And latent under the roof of the womb
The new life growing keeps time.

Birth and death, in shuddering lonely
Pangs alike, and not in this only:
Not a parallel, but the same process
Waxing or waning into a new place.
Willed or involuntary, who can say?
The wild source being hidden far away.
Such tender durable stuff the new-born flesh,
Such brittle durable the dying, that outlasts the wish
To live. And past all wish or hope of ours,
O, past our entreaties and our tears
Are these twin movements, ebb and flow
In a life persistent as the green under the snow.

To Mark Time

For Benedict Ridler

To mark time is not to move:
Only the unkept hours drip from the clock
Or pull at the cord coiled in its groove,
The marker moveless, and the change illusion.

The sundial shows only delightful hours,
Nor seems to move although the shadow changes.
You who watch the moment, standing still
For the peace which, always coming, never will,

Look how this child marks time within his flesh
In multiplying cells whose life is movement;
Hold him in your arms and so enmesh
The moving moment, promise and fulfilment.

So nurse the joy of which the smiles speak;
See how his lashes, like the sundial's finger
Measuring only light – the heavenly light –
Mark this time in shadows on his cheek.

Views of the North Coast

(Cornwall)

The yellow mustard-field and green cliff,
Bright and flat as a racegame landscape,
Smooth coves and upward combes with a stiff
Thatch of sea-shorn oaks, these
For the estuary, that smooths the brimming seas
Below the Bar where late the mermaids sang;
And oyster-catchers, snatching the light,
Fly in a black-and-white cartoon before
The wind – these for the estuary, endless days
That silt in centuries against the shore.

Seaward, the great capes with foreheads pressed
Against the tide; after the storm
The sun like a red ship rolls in the breakers westward,
Ridge upon ridge the steep seas
Rush on the rocks, Alps that flame and freeze
Endlessly pouring down the slope of the world,
And flecks of foam like gulls in a flock
Catch the last light, until the red ship sinks.
Then still the unseen monstrous waters pour
In centuries against the crumbling shore.

Romney Marsh

For Kenneth and Millie Swan

Crossing this country, stranger, remember
    Your strange beginnings:
How you lay senseless under the tide
    Who now stride
Upright, and hear the lark and linnet.
    This ground you tread
That nurtures the white coin-bearing sheep
    Once could keep
The muddy sea-mouse, hiding a sunset
    In his hairs,
Or the dark sticky grapes of the sea;
    This that is now mellow and gay
With the yellow horned poppy and bugloss
    Felt the waves toss.
They huddle now like sheep to the pens
    Of wooden piles:
How little divides them from the soil
    Our fathers stole,
And from you, stranger, who remember
    Your wild beginnings;
To whom the wild gull complains,
To whom the sea grumbles in its chains.

To a Magician on her Retirement

For O.W.

Enchanters may relinquish
    That which is not their own:
The art to raise the tempest
    Or quicken the dawdling moon –
These would be foreign powers
    Coiled in a word or a sign,
But what shall we say of yours
    Within the spirit grown?
The natural magnificence –

Dead, these niggardly days,
Till you revived the forgotten Prince
With his unpredictable ways –
The gardener's green finger
For planting, and the skill
To teach the living creature
Its own secret will;
To make of a house, a symbol,
To make of a school, a seal
Marked in the heart for a lifetime,
These arts cannot fail.
For these are native powers,
You cannot lay them down,
You must remain a magician
As long as your days remain.
Then what is the secret knowledge,
The word and symbol? love;
The hidden force and motive,
The cell and movement? love.

We who are your debtors
What can we say or give?
Beggars – yes, but beggars may
Be liberal of love.
So what you taught, may you receive,
And what you gave, have.

Words Commissioned for Music

The rails and seas depart our loves;
The heart a martyr
Every hour to the cruel grooves
Finds that sudden death is a necessary art.

Stillness on the crest of a wave
Is love's rest:
Time breaks, but seabird lovers have
In vanishing hollows their renewing nest.

As, the sad and livelong day,
  Seas give
Water to skies that skies repay,
Love rains returning; so by our deaths we live.

Bach's B Minor Mass

'Faith discerns not the images but what the images signify:
and yet we cannot discern it except *through* the images. We
cannot by-pass the images to seize and imageless truth.'
                                    AUSTIN FARRER: *The Glass of Vision*

There is no word but what the poem says
Nor any image but what the music does.

Credo: does it rehearse what Christian men believe?
The beat defines it and the chords receive.
Sanctus: does it cry to the unattainable height?
Only through the lung's pressure and the bow's bite.
The infinite descent of the Incarnation
Falls in the strings toward the Desolation –
A pain once known, at once to be assuaged,
For the Resurrection is to come at the turning of the page.

Yet with the final phrase we fall from grace.
Though memory may describe the voice of stars –
Those noble and night-riding spheres
Sounding for ever in this holy gyre –
Or angels of sound that upward and downward pass
On a serpentine stair in sempiternal peace,
The wonder eludes these legends, yet the ear
Has faithful echoes in its choir.

It is not to see all heaven before one's eyes
But to become the very stuff of heaven
To live within this music. Yet it dies?
O not the music, but we die from it, as even
Its author did, who never heard it wholly played.
The ear is mortal, but the heaven it had
Is truth, no likeness, and its bliss, of God.

Travellers' Tales

'Struggling for an image on the track
Of the moving Zodiac'
                    W.B. YEATS

1

The fear of death beside the green boy growing,
With his manhood puts out curious blooms:
To end with honour kept, and wasted –
This is the fear that drives him over hills of glass
Or into art-schools. O to have found that state,
Shunned in the bedside explanation, sought in books –
    The Black Tulip,
The Cloister and the Hearth, and such; that state
Of which the travellers' tales can only tantalize;
The inconceivable creating place
Between the temporal cliff and eternal sea,
Between the cliff and nursing arm of the sea, where
The storm is heard as peace, where body and spirit
Compose their quarrel, rock and water are one:
The body to keep, the spirit to lose, its pride,
The spirit given in the creating charity,
The body justified with all its flaws.

Where the storm is heard as peace.
Then was his fear a longing too for death
Which satisfied has put an end to fear?
Host still to the parasite, he sees it
With blossom shrivelled and diminished power
Though in its dreadful hour to be effective:
Once lost for love, he can bear to lose his breath.

2

As the moon draws the waters
As the moon-drawn waters come
Over the sea-world, up to the sea-wall,
So she draws her pleasure home.

What shall we learn? At six o'clock
The battle begins. The longing fills
The world, up to the brim of stillness
Where the wheel hangs before it falls.

The Golden Bird 85

Gently move, that the wheel may not
Fall too soon, gently move
That the storm may not break too quickly,
Though the breaking-point is love.

The element of change is stillness,
Till it fall in lashing leaves
In storming waters, here unbroken
Love, to be broken, forever lives.

3

There lives forever, but we fall away.
As the jacinth coast lay marvellous in a dream
And so must remain, but lost perhaps for ever,
We have no certain promise to return
Although we have done so. And words are powerless.
To pause for an image in the dance is to lose
The dance itself: intractable to words
The extremes of the abstract and sensual alike.
What then remains? The mental proof:
By faith not by feeling is ecstasy commemorated.
Also, it may be, the living child,
But the child was not shaped by the joy of its making.
Love has other places, and is implacable,
Who can predict the luck of his embrace?
Only in love is the storm heard as peace,
Leave then to love the recapitulation.

Propitious Time

'Every generation is equidistant from eternity.'
RANKE, quoted by HERBERT BUTTERFIELD

Does Love that issues in a rosy boy
Find in this fruit the reason of his being?
And harvest his true season, not the bud the shoot
Or petal time the very prime of joy?

Confused in freedom is what he did intend.
Incarnate in a moment of their kindness
Those childless lovers also gave him flesh:
Love did not mock, but made the cause the end.

But we to escape the burden of his peace
Look ceaselessly toward some future heaven:
As if our race moved to a far perfection
Belittle the past, excuse our own disease.

For history or souls each hour's the prime,
Not by itself but in itself perfected;
Most favoured each the eternal light's encounter
Reached at the moment of propitious time.

Columbine and Larkspur

Six doves or dancers
Crowd on a stem with feet for balance
Pointed askance:
Or cones of glass
Or cockle hats hung on a hidden thread.
If there were doves of yellow and red
If songs were buds
                    If birds had
The stillness of sap and flight were frozen...
Here on a stem
Move
         The dancers but will not leave.
If there were doves
This colour and dolphin-birds this blue...
The garden breaks
In a thousand stained-glass fragments. Who
Sees and makes
                    The ordered picture
With these above and these below
That these should fly and these should grow,
With leads to fix

Wings and calyx
And keeps the clue?
But now
        They bow
Set and exchange as dancers do.

Piero della Francesca

The body is not fallen like the soul:
For these are godlike, being
Wholly of flesh, and in that being whole.
Founded on earth, they seem to be built not painted –
These huge girls, the mountain marble and
The valley clays were mixed for them,
The cleanness of lavender and the coolness of sand,
Also the tints of the deep sea;
And from the sea were made
The shell-like apse, and the pillars that echo each other
As waves do, in the Virgin's grey colonnade.

This gentle Jerome, with his Christ nailed
To the brown hill behind his head,
In speech with a stolid Donor, could not be
(Surely) by Manichaean doubts assailed;
In bodily peace this Solomon is wise:
Nothing is tortured, nothing ethereal here,
Nor would transcend the limits of material
Being, for in the flesh is nothing to fear
And nothing to despise.
The singing choir is winged, but who would wish
To fly, whose feet may rest on earth?
Christ with his banner, Christ in Jordan's water,
Not humbled by his human birth.

Venetian Scene

(S. Giorgio Maggiore)

Fill the piazza with blue water
And gaze across domestic seas
From church to church. The tide is tame,
The streets look firm with floating marble.
Who made the sea ride in the city?
Movement is all a floating. Ride
The idle tide that smooths the steps:
Now statues ride in the blue air,
Light floats across the white façade
And seaweed over the marble stairs.

Backgrounds to Italian Paintings: Fifteenth Century

Look between the bow and the bowstring, beneath
The flying feet of confederate angels,
Beyond old Montefeltro's triumph seat –
There the delectable landscape lies
Not furtive, but discreet:
It is not hiding, but withholds the secret.
What do the calm foreground figures know of it?
(Suffering martyrdom, riding a triumph
With a crowd of nymphs and Loves about the car)
What do they know of the scenes wherein they are?

The knees of the hills rise from wreaths of sleep,
The distant horsemen glimmer; the pigment fading
Has turned the juniper-green to brown;
And there the river winds away for ever.

We ourselves have walked those hills and valleys
Where the broom glows and the brittle rock-rose,
Combes are cool with chestnut and plains with poplar:
The juniper there was green – we have been
There, but were not given the secret,
Did not find our rest.

So give this land a stranger's look at best.

Later the landscape stole the picture, the human
Figures were banished, and with the figures vanished
From every natural scene the look of secrets.
So it seems that the figures held the clue.
Gaze at the story boldly as children do –
The wonder awaits you, cornerwise, but never
Full in the face; only the background promises,
Seen through the purple cones at the edge of the eye
And never to be understood:
The sleep-wreathed hills, the ever-winding river.

Deus Absconditus

'...so shall we be drawn by that sight from Ignorance and Sin...
But by what cords? The cords of a man, and the cords of Love.'
THOMAS TRAHERNE

I selfish and forsaken do still long for you
God for whom I was born and should have died:
Like lovers over miles and miles of sea
I lean my heart toward my comfort uselessly;
Did man or God weep out this sundering tide?

Cut off each sense, withdraw to the inmost secret place:
This God absconds from every promised land.
To shrink like a mollusc and to find no grace
This is the lot his lovers face.

And yet the worst is, not to seek you; yet the worst
Is not to know our lack of you. O, Love,
By what cords will you draw us? As at first
The cords of a man? Not splendour but the penal flesh
Taken for love, that moves us most.

Who breaks his tryst in a passionate ritual
May burn in a dry tree, a cold poem,
In the weak limbs of a child, so instant and perpetual,
In the stranger's face of a father dying,
Tender still but all the while departing.

Here he is endured, here he is adored.
And anywhere. Yet it is a long pursuit,
Carrying the junk and treasure of an ancient creed,
To a love who keeps faith by seeming mute
And deaf, and dead indeed.

'I who am here dissembled'

To T.S. Eliot on his Sixtieth Birthday

Poetry is, as you said, a *mug's game*.
   The poem, written, is lost: may earn a wage
   But cannot grow, or comfort old age.
Saints move on the unbroken beam,
   But poets look with a refractory eye
On decomposing light, and need to stray.
   The work is restless, restless to refuse;
   At last even the self dissembled dies.

But where the wretched bones were laid, the tree
   Softly rustled its leaves like a child clapping,
   And a bird sang out of the juniper, such a singing
Stilled the world and earned its glory's fee
   (To break the sorcery and to find relief)
   The gold chain of love and the millstone of grief.

O Love Answer

O Love, answer the hammering heart:
   Only in love we live; then prove
That quickening good, take your own part,
   Show us that all your modes are one.

Go where the frustrate lovers lie
   On earth that gives back no caress,
Trying to calm in a chthonic pain
   Their howling torment: raise and bless.

Appease with just and holy ends
    Their tenderness; their need to give
Turn to some profit – what are their wounds
But mere irrelevance to Love?

To those whose inner wars forbade
    The deed of love, grant a release.
The satisfied and then betrayed
    Endure the greater torment, since
Love is not blind, but worships still
The glory in the mad and cruel.
    Only the Cross can justify
    Their folly and their agony.

Last, visit the lucky in love.
    Make them as strangers, yet possessing
All the skill that use can give.
    Let ecstasy convert the soul
At last, restore the mystery
    Their raptures have burnt up, his ways
Instruct with spendthrift power and be
    The light that leaps through all her house.

Then be their envoy to ask forgiveness
    From the unsatisfied, a pardon
For their luck and for their ease.
    O reconcile the twin directions
Not at the infinite point, but this.
    We do not believe in the happy ending.
It must be now, for pain and peace
    In present commerce, one perfection.

As, in poetry, rise and fall
    Naming the measure, can exchange
Or take each other's semblance well,
    Marked from a different point in time,
So might one measure hold us all:
    All was in ecstasy begun,
Yet the poor heart beats pain for ever –
    Prove that your terrible ways are one.

The Filament

For R.S.

'All desire delight in the same way as they desire good: and yet
they desire delight by reason of the good and not conversely.'
AQUINAS

December shoots tell us that the crocus burns;
Above the waxen weeping flames the wick.

I have bewailed the wounds I gave,
I have known the sensual torment,
I have seen a spinster's solitude
Wait like a wolf beside my door –
Love was there yet was not these.

I have been rocked in affection's cradle,
I have shocked the sheaves of achievement,
I have numbered my golden children –
Love was there yet was not these.

O flame above the waxen tears,
O fire within the glowing bulb –
So love in its passion burns,
Either with peace, either with pain.
The filament of flower or lamp,
The thread that guides and is the flame,
Their life is in their shining, not
In the elements their light combines;
The wire's resistance makes more white
The candid light wherein it shines.

Blood Transfusion Centre

'He that gives, let him do it with simplicity.'

But which of us, waiting to offer his oblation
Can look at what he does with entire simplicity?
For between the lifeblood and the dying man
Science interposes its marvellous devices,
Isolating microbes, magnifying cells,
Testing, sealing, measuring, preserving.

So here we stand, in a queue for pure love
(Or it may be, for guilt, or it may be, for pride):
Shop-soiled housewives, typists and gardeners,
Lads and old soldiers – we look at each other
And wonder that health could spring from such complexions,
That such or such a man should design such a gift.
Yet each in his veins is offering the ichor,
Each has entertained the secret vision
Of health by his sickness; of life by his loss.

And here are the couches, with their patient figures
Whose blood is now flowing; and beyond these
The resting figures; and the cups of tea
Tasting of ether. The design is forgotten
In the details of performance: in chatting with the nurse,
In a sore vein, a thumping heart, a wearisome waiting.

To see this as godlike in the rest is to burden
The self who is one; to belittle it here
Belittles it in them. To give for those we love
Is natural as breathing, but should we not be hypocrites
To say that we loved this abstraction of Humanity?
The pelican's breast was not pierced for a stranger.
The man who gives his seed to beget for another
Creates he knows not what. The man who gives his blood
Restores he knows not what. We call in question
Such dangerous goodwill as moves in the first,
But what of the second? Who would have the right
To pretend to the impartial love of a god
And divide himself, not for a man but for Men?

Dindrane who gave her blood to succour a sick woman
And died so, did truly die another's death;
But the woman had her part – to live another's life,
And pain is as hard to relinquish as to bear.
So, toward a presence not abstract though not seen,
Both move, giver and receiver, through darkness.
(We speak of Love as blind, because his day is dark to us.)

The queue moves forward. Humbly we consider –
Humbly and with amazement –
'He that gives, let him do it with simplicity.'

The Constellation[1]

Silent the Lyre that streams among the stars
And lulled is the fierce Lion:
So is Orpheus' torment turned
To memory and peace
Pricked out in stars a counterpoint that cannot sound.

So fixed, so quiet, the family constellations
Are memories of love or hate:
Yet each has had its hot creation
When with new sons the old forms fade
Before the calm irrevocable past is made.

These grow and sing: with their sweet jangling cries
The bickering soaring children
Elder with younger jostle for place.
Their milky light, their all-regarding gaze
Has travelled here a billion miles of space:
Distant they are, not fixed, nor frozen, nor at peace.

[1] 'The Family Constellation' is, I understand, Adler's term.

Picking Pears

Nor heaven, nor earth, a state between,
  Whose walls of leaves
Weave in a chequer of dark and bright
The falling sky; whose roofs of green
Are held by ropes and chains and beams of light.

Regenerate summer hangs in the trees:
  Hours of sunshine
  Charged the cells, and spread the loot
So thick about us that we seize
  Even the leaves dissembling globes of fruit.

Strange that we only in harvest season
  Borrow from birds
  These parks of air, these visions over the fence:
Not the flat view of soaring reason
  But a sharper angle, the height of exalted sense.

We enter only to despoil:
  Solaced and proud
Though barren twigs are left behind,
Through a weft of leaves we sink to the soil,
But summer's nimbus shrivels on the rind.

Mare Nostrum

Changeable beast with rumpled fur of foam
She plunges along the land,
Held by a moonstring, yet by solid rock
Hardly contained.

She is nothing to look at – only clouds and light
Contrive her vanishing jewels,
Her melting zircon and her solid agate.
If you would see her nature, watch

Those palpitating globes within the pool
More transparent yet more firm than mist:
Her life is a bubble of nothing, cool
Nothing, and like the jellyfish persists.

This yielding overpowers. All in her likeness
Are flutes and whorls in shell and rock and sand,
The conch full of her music,
The water-colours of wentletrap and fan.

And men who chose the shore, aeons ago,
Still spin their memories of her into glass,
Whose splinters worn by water seem to be
Solid green fragments of the sea.

But solid forms renounce her. As for men,
Though other vertebrates return,
Choice of dry land has lost her, let them swim
Each summer through her waves, they never find home.

The lost sea-nature. If her deeps are still,
She has given to men who yearn and may not return to them
Only the restless surface,
The quiet buried away,
The sunset shattered across the rocks in spray.

The Speech of the Dead

News of the dead is heard through words of the living.
After a casual phrase
Sometimes we burn with tears to recognize
Familiar words of the dead,
And Never again Never again cries against the loving greeting;
News of the dead, but by the living heard as
Dead news, and no true meeting.

No twittering ghosts, they speak as they always did,
But through our lips. Do they pursue and haunt us,
Or is it we who haunt them with the past, and will not rid
Their glory of that obsessive ghost?

O, in the sharp pale beams of the winter air
We seem to breathe their element, and the cold stir
About the brain is their interior speech.
They haunt us, and we them,
But it is our sad yearning that keeps them out of reach.

Those words out of the past that gave us pain
For the present, those are still our spirits' exchange,
But sounding through them now, most deeply felt,
A death- and a life-time's loss and gain.

The blind to each of their four senses add
A little skill and so atone for the fifth.
Might we, for that blind lack in not being dead,
Atone by greater silence and the skill
To guess and be still.
Not to imagine them sharing this or that
Our temporal activity, and turn
Their supernatural state to ours, but
To know them as they are through what we know they were;
And in that glory of love to learn
Words of the dead through living lips a prayer.

Michelangelo in the Accademia

(Florence)

Perfect in every part, the David
Reigns a heedless king of being:
All is said and all is freed.
But down the hall on either side
The prisoners strain toward existence:
They strain against the vice of stone
And agonise against the vice
Of shapelessness, and start the chain
Of atoms battering through the brain
To crack the clodding world apart.

And last of all the heavy Christ
Borne upward by his groaning creatures,
Bound within his death of stone,
That death in stone but partly done.
Undone for ever, yet the part
Strangely suffices, while we feel
The final truth in all our limbs
As growing outwards from the heart.

On a Picture by Michele da Verona

of Arion as a boy riding upon a dolphin

Here is the foreign cliff and the fabled sea,
But where is the wealthy youth we read of,
Whose music charmed the dolphins, that they bore him
Out of the reach of murderous men
To Taenarus (green-marbled Matapan)?

When he played, surely the waves he filled
With music froze, and common time was stilled
As at the intricate measure of Orpheus' song,
Past in a flash and yet a lifetime long.

But here is no frozen trance: a naked urchin
Shouting dissolves the world in waves of sound;
The cavern of the winds is in his throat,
And all comes pouring out of that primal cave
In notes that harden into hills or seas.

Out of one source, brown billows and brown land;
The gondola darts like a fish, the spiny men
Are vertebrates of sea or shore, and the castle
Caught on the cliff-top like an ark is stranded.

Astride upon a winking dolphin's neck
Arion shouts and sings, his yellow cloak
Fills with the wind;
His viol is carved with the head of a rakish cat;
He is a little noisy brat;
Also, he has the world at his command.

Villanelle for the Middle of the Way

When we first love, his eyes reflect our own;
When mirrors change to windows we can see;
Seeing, we know how much is still unknown.

Was it a trite reflection? What is shown
When we gaze deep begins the mystery:
When we first love, his eyes reflect our own.

Neither of us could cast the first stone,
And to forgive is tender. 'Now,' thought we,
'Seeing, we know.' How much was still unknown

We later learnt. But by forgiveness grown –
As Blake discovered – apt for eternity,
Though in first love his eyes reflect our own.

What was the crime for which you would atone
Or could be crime now between you and me
Seeing we know how much is still unknown?

I know you now by heart not eyes alone,
Dearer the dry than even the green tree.
When we first love, his eyes reflect our own,
Seeing, we know how much is still unknown.

The Golden Bird[1]

Note. 'Truth has no greater enemy than verisimilitude and likelihood', 1754, quotes the dictionary. I have aimed at truth but not likelihood, and the poem depends upon its success in making the reader accept its time and place as *now* and *here*, and in making the diverse mythical traditions upon which it draws become 'domesticated into power'.

What is so strange as a bird?
What is so swift as thought?
What is so calm as the flesh in its glory?

'Trees that grow by windows are   The King
The space and flight of seasons to those that lie within: speaks:
Soul escapes from feverish body,
Clad in cool leaves to glide among the boughs
Where beams of bark and healing light   The
Support the fretted sky.   Apple
This apple tree beside the palace windows   Tree
Was a sensible world to me as I lay ill
Through which I lived by proxy.
Its fruit possessed the flavour of the cool moon's shining,
The taste of the hot sun was on the rind;
And while the apples sustained me
My sickness stayed like a watchdog by the door
But did not take possession.

'I the king lay sick,
I showed in my body the malady of my people:
Much knowledge, little wonder.
No myths were born from us – the more we thought
The less our thought sustained us;
Caring only for How, we were careless of What;
Nervous and yet despising the bounds of the flesh,
Our bodies had no peace.
And as my kingdom suffered this impoverishment,
So with a slow anaemia my blood was whitened,
A dying delayed by the apples,
Delayed, but never cured.

[1] See 'The Golden Bird', Grimm's *Household Tales*, No. 57; and 'The Greek Princess and the Young Gardener', Joseph Jacobs' *More Celtic Fairy Tales*, No. 37. Another version is in J.F. Campbell's *West Highland Tales*.

'And then the bird began its thefts.
Waking one night, I watched it at work in the tree
Golden among the moon-glazed fruit
And flying off, an apple held in its beak.
Every night an apple
While every night the watchers slept,
The gardener's sons in turn, until the third one
Watched with waking eyes, and fired –
And in the morning they brought me
A heavy feather, solid gold.
Then from the tree I heard this song,
As though the bird had left it hanging
Among the leaves, an aeolian harp for the wind.

' "The gold of flowers is
      Light as feathers
Gold-dust alyssum
      Lichen that weathers
On rosy walls
And the pale powder
      Of the spring sallows.
The gold of air is
      Pollen and petal
The gold of earth
      A heavy metal:
Air is my element
      Earth my matrix
My flight is feathered
      With heavy ore
But light as flowerdust
      I soar:
I steal men's good
      And arouse their greed
So that the Kingdom
      Suffers their need.

O what a happy bird am I!"

'If I pursued the bird for greed
It was for greed of healing and wholeness:
I was not able to rest in my half-health
But goaded to pursue my vanished powers.

Though others made my journey, all their fatigues
And flights were mine, loss and success were mine.
The gardener's elder sons, curmudgeonly boys,
Each in turn set out, each in turn
Met the Fox at the gate of the palace grounds
Gentle and still in the heavy evening light
Gazing steadily at them.
Here was a beautiful strange beast, and therefore
(Being as they were, and in the common run
Of elder sons) they fired at it, but missed.
For which the Fox returned them good advice.
This they mislaid in the next town, so losing
The search, the bird, themselves.

'The third son, no Galahad for a quest
Was yet a humble studious boy,
Unapt to make comparisons of talent or reward.
Meeting the Fox, he also took it for a beast,
But since he respected its nature, heard its words.
He went with it as quietly as Tobit with his angel.
And while he went, I waited:
Waited in sickness, where I dreamt, and prayed.

      'There is a spring
      Hidden in a garden
      Icy in the hot sun
      Flowing in the frost:
      My lips approach
      These waters in dreams
      But they taste on the tongue
      As the savourless drops
      From chalk-furred kettles.
      Crisp apples, restore
      To the spring its crystal,
      Son, be our saviour.'

'I, the third son, departed from my father's house.   The
Nursed in rich woods, flattered by reflecting lakes,   Third
With careful lawns as close as corduroy,   Son
With kerchief sapphire seen through a dark yew alley,   speaks
And graceful bridges which are only follies –
So rural palaces, in cities,

Deceive the street-sore eyes of urban men
Who seek the fields. Deceive, and also solace them.
In such a place I grew.
My father, loving the elegant pretence,
Watered the ground with colours of the sea,
With lithospermum, flag and flax and gentian,
And through those blue deeps blazed his mineral fires –
Purple and coral of heliotrope and heuchera.
I had no skill at the artifice; he sighed at me,
But kept me working, and every day was summer,
Until they sent me after the robber Bird.

His
Journey

'I climbed the hill, through tunnels
Of tall holly and laurel,
Past the tree of heaven
And past the catalpa tree,
And at the summit, where the fence
Divides the quiet woods
From the screaming road of traffic,
I turned to look at the palace
Wearing its skin of stucco
Pitted and smeared with smoke.
There as I stood, I felt him,

He meets
the Fox

The Fox, gazing at me,
And seeing him, stooped for a stone –
This from a boy's habit,
For I felt no wish to kill him.
He did not move, but gazed on,
A rufus beast, with steady human eyes.
I waited for him to speak.
Did his words reach my ear
Or sound within my brain?
I cannot recall his voice,
And yet I knew his meaning.
I mounted on his tail. We flew
Over the road, and down the hill called Spaniards,
Past the Bull and Bush,
And into Chessington Park.
There flowers and terraces are laid
For the eyes of a vanished house:
A house in a cloak of darkness
To which the paths are leading,

That watches the herd at hide and seek in the trees.
There above the dawdling lilies of the ditch
We saw the Bird go flitting,
And by the light of its wings
The house appeared for an instant,
Perfect above the terraces
With its warm life outgoing
In paths that spread like rays.
An instant – then was gone.
The Bird flew over the Heath
Where the muddy little stream is make-believe for a river,
Past the paddling children,
Past the sprouting allotments,
Till we lost it in the Suburb.
There the Fox delayed and spoke again.
"We are now come," it said, "to a strange place: Hamp-
Here man is to be orderly, genteel and prosperous,   stead
Fecund, a lover of flowers, and keep no fowls.   Garden
Here is High spire, Low dome, and Quaker garden,   Suburb
But there is no public-house
And no class-feeling, for here there is only one class
And one design for living;
In spring it seems a sky-borne city
Laid upon rosy clouds of blossoming trees.
Now the tormenting Bird
To this of all unlikely spots
Has brought its lawless bill.
There in that house you will find it:
The family lies asleep,
But use all care, and do not dare disturb it,
It perches where it wills:
Carry it off as you find it."

'I approach the costly cottage
Of regulation Tudor:
The rain jumped up from the roof like fluttering birds;
The door flew open before me,
I heard the inmates breathing,
And the dark hall was lit
By the glow, more gold than candles
More bright than incandescence,
Of the marvellous Bird, which hung in an old wire meat-safe.

It also seemed to be sleeping,
Its head under its wing.
Near by on a table lay a splendid cage:
It seemed sheer folly to leave it
And carry the Bird in a safe
Like a fly-blown joint of meat;
So, forgetting the Fox's words,

The Bird
is lost

I lifted it softly out.
At that the provoking creature uttered a squawk
That raised the lid of my skull
And brought the family down –
Father, mother and children –
Howling Thief and threatening me with prison.
Not that the Bird was theirs,
Nor did the golden cage entice it, only
The old wire safe the children kept, somewhere,
To use for a diving-bell or a rocket to the moon,
The saving makeshift in a wealthy house.

'But now the earth spun round like a bobbin,
The stars shook swords and clashed,
And I lost myself, for when I opened my eyes
All was dark and vacant about me.
Only a voice within my skull said this:

'"Who looks where he should be blind,
Who tries to gild the guiltless,
Loses and leaves the treasure behind.
Yet virtue out of his fault
Yet riches from his loss
By the irrational laws of love are brought.
What can bewilder like winged gold
Yet what is so swift as thought?"

'I stretched out my hand and felt the fell of the Fox.
"Forgive," I began – but London was lessening below
    us,
A table of golden crumbs for celestial birds,
And the wind pressed my breath back into my throat,
I was suffocating with too much air.
I clung to the brush that supported me;
We shot towards the height

As though we meant to be fixed among the stars
To make a new constellation.
We overtook the message of light that sped
From the earth an hour ahead of us,
Then travelled with it as a plane that keeps its beam
Or a note in tune, with an even cool vibration.
So we came, in no measurable time,
To a place where three ways and two seasons met –
In spring at the edge of Oxford.

' "Here," said the Fox, "is a city of screaming tyres,   Oxford:
Where lorries piled with motor-shells   the Plain
Fly like clumsy Maybugs through the streets,
And the river drumbles past exotic barges.
The smoke of learning rises with the river-mists
And spires like funnels carry praise to heaven.
Thin and rare is the rising praise
But the heavenly thought descends in flesh and blood.
Once with tremendous wings vanning the sky   Pegasus
It seemed a flying horse, and prayed for, came
To kill the chimaera of men's dismal fears;
Then sprang, like a diver rising from the depths, to
    Olympus,·
Throwing its rider, who would have ridden to heaven
But had not learnt its horsemanship.
That speedy power feeds and drinks in this city:
Some have seen it here, but none has taken it.
Nor are you yet able to ride it:
Do not mount, but bring it by the bridle, softly."

'I crossed the bridge, with the whirling wrack of traffic.
The sky was laid below me in azure anemones,
The willows wept against the sun like rainbows
And punts as lazy as clouds slipped by beneath.
I came to the double gateway   Botanical
Where the Stuarts guard the tranquil garden,   Gardens
The chimes fall among rare plants like rain
And blackened ashlar walls debar
The rabble of prams and all disorderly persons.
A wolf and boar of stone
Sat snarling back on their haunches,

And the Horse of the wind-outpacing thought
Quietly fed there, tasting
The luculent waxen blooms
Of the leafless magnolia tree.

'I approached it softly:
Its mane was like the flowing stone
Of ripples on a Greek *stele*,
The sculptured waves of thought.
Its wings that could beat like waves were folded,
Its eyes the intuitive crystal, veiled,
Its phallus the power of creation, sleeping.
It turned and watched me calmly,
While I, on fire to master it
And once again forgetful,
Put my hand on its back, prepared to mount.
Whereat it lifted its head
And neighed to the top of Tom Tower.

'On that, a white-haired man stepped out from the gate,
Who spoke to me – softly, but his words were cold
And more deadly than anger:
Of how one could not hope to master the truth
Without a lifetime's labour; even then
Only the few . . . and then I heard no more;
The light of my own being was lost to me,
Utterly lost, my Self a burnt-out shred
Blown in the gutter, hardly worth a search.

'But yet I called to the Fox
As a child in the night, or a lover
Who calls one name though he knows he cannot be
    heard.
Then I felt myself caught up,
The air was keening about me
As I clung to the fell of the Fox in the blackness
Speeding through the sky.
And I heard, "Again you have lost
    But out of loss comes gain
    Though all against man's deserts."

'We flew above seas and mountains,
And Time was streaming out like a banner behind us.
I shut my eyes and slept,
And when I awoke, we stood before an altar   Arezzo:
Where painted walls on either side   Piero
Portrayed the legend of the Genuine Cross.   della
There enormous horses, noble girls,   Francesca
Were built like towers on the shining earth,
And colour in a visible fugue
Resolved in space the perplexities of time:
The death of Adam, watched
By withered Eve and solemn leaning sons,
The Queen of Sheba's vision by the bridge,
And portly Solomon by his porphyry temple;
The agonies of battle
Calm in the intricate pattern of perspective;
And there beneath a steep and chequered town
The excavated Cross performing wonders,
While dwarf and peasant watched without surprise.

' "Look," said the Fox, "look inwardly,
For here the flesh is not
Despised, is not diseased:
As here the form is known through colour,
So is the spirit through flesh.
Not only look but gaze,
And gazing grow to what you see, seeing possess it."

'I gazed at Piero's choir
Where once he laid on the molten universe
The cool moulds of the Five Regular Bodies
(The triangle, dodecahedron and the rest).
I gazed, and as I gazed
I found my feet descending
From the brown humped hill
To where the Queen of Sheba
Under the curls of an olive
Knelt, and her women waited.
Green and murrey and russet their gowns
Under an olive sky. And one   The Lady
Whose white cloak hung back stiffly from her shoulders
Greeted me gravely. This was my thought:

'O marvel of marmoreal shoulders
O coolness of peace in the carven face:
Her neck is a doric pillar
Her brow is the arch's keystone...

'But I heard the Fox's words:
"Do not let her turn, do not let her turn to her companions
Weighing the loss with the profit
Remembering her first perfection.
She must not turn her head."

'I moved to take her hand –
And there I stood in the chapel
Beside a living girl
Whose likeness still above with hand outstretched
Leaned to the kneeling Queen.
I did not doubt her touch
(Who doubts the force of the wind
Or turbulence of seas?)
But kept – more real than common sense – this dream for a
        lifetime's waking.
"Beloved," I said, "will you come?
And do not turn your head.
Until you have given me all, you can gain nothing;
Until I have ruled your will, I cannot free it.
Do not weigh me against your loss, so light as I am,
Do not betray me, in my first assay,
Only because I love, obey,
And do not turn your head."

'She did not turn again
But came with me to where the Fox was waiting.
I took her in my arms,
We mounted on his brush
And threaded skies, the miles
Melting into minutes
The minutes into miles,
And as we crossed the English coast
The Fox lifted his head and called.
Then over the horizon flying
The winged Horse approached,
Swift as wild swans but soundless,

The light streamed back from its shoulders
And flowed in a wake of flame.
Then from the opposite quarter
The golden Bird, whose passing
Left the clouds still glowing
As the west smoulders after the sun has sunk.

'We flew, while these encircling us
Wrote upon the dark sky
In a script of fire;
And came at last to the wooded entrance
Where first the Fox awaited me.

'"Child," he said, "you are now come home   The
After the flights, the loss and gain,   Return
Having your trophies about you.
Go, give back his wasted powers to the King,
And health through him to his people.
He being sonless shall
Receive a son from you
Raised to you by this Lady
To wear the rays of the crown."

'So we went down again through the laurel tunnels.
Close to the gate I saw two men half hidden,
Who as we passed came softly after.
"There are my brothers," I said, "who started the search
And never returned." "Well," said the Fox, "let them follow;
They are hoping to share in the glory,
And if there is glory, what does it matter who shares it?"

'Coming to the palace, we found the pale King
Waiting before the door, with all his household.
I knelt to him, and the Bird flew to his shoulder,
The Horse drew tamely near,
And the Lady knelt to kiss his hand
But he prevented her, kissing her forehead.

'"Now the King shall have health
And his land shall feast upon light.
But first before the day breaks,
Dear son," said the Fox to me,

"If I have brought you safely through
The lonely interstellar dark
And the crowded fields of anger,
And if the deeds I demanded
Though for the King you did them,
Led to your own good,
Now I must ask a stranger task,
Not for your own profit,
Not for your own peace,
But for mercy alone."

' "Ask," I said. But when he spoke, my heart
Crashed like a falling 'plane.

'He lifted his paw and said with a pleading look:
"Under that elm tree you will find an axe
Forgotten by the woodmen.
Take it and cut off my head."
                              I could not answer,
But fell on my knees and prayed him with my tears
To make his words unsaid.

' "If you're so squeamish, let me carve the joint."
This from my eldest brother standing near,
Who would have fetched the axe, but I prevented him.
"No one shall touch him but I. Yet O, dear master,
Why? Is our charge of hatred then so lethal
That love must die of it if he would discharge us?
And if, since suicide's forbidden, love
Requires a murderer for his work of mercy,
How can the murderer forgive?"

'But all the while I spoke, I knew it was useless.
The Fox said no more, but looked at me,
And then lay down, his head at my feet.

'I could not move, but the Lady, bringing the axe
Held it out to me sadly. I took it from her,
Then I measured the distance, shut my eyes,
And in a kind of frenzy swung it
Heavily down and struck.
                              On that

A great wave in my brain broke, and I fainted.
But while I lay half dead I heard this song –
Again I could not tell if the world breathed it
Or the words welled from within.

   ' "O man, the child of fuming stars
   And victim of created light,
   You know your plight but not God's meaning:
   Love is his meaning; learn it well
   Seeing this image of his pure goodwill.
   The strange disguise that guilty fears
   Had hung about his form is shed
   By the blow that freed its own hatred.
   Now is his meaning plain
   And truth not from a well but flagrant from his forehead
      shines."

'The Fox's hide lay shrivelled at my feet,
And as I raised my eyes
I saw a tall man, above whose shoulders
The sun seemed to be rising
So bright a light shone round him.
To look into his eyes was
To see a flame burning through dark water,
And to come near him
Was to be warmed at the fire of his kindness.
The Bird perched on his shoulder
(And now for the first time I heard it singing –
A song that pierced as though its notes were ice),
His hand lay on the neck of the winged Horse.

'We stood for a while bewildered;
Then he smiled, and joy burst in my heart
Like the sudden opening of an iris
Whose dark petals unfurl
To show their golden rays.
And I felt that fear and sorrow
Could never be more than names heard in a dream.
As when, within a sombre church
At the sudden shining of the sun outside
The walls and windows glow,
Not as with light reflected

But as if they beamed out of some secret store,
So at his smile we glowed, all of us there;
And all looked round astonished
To see the sudden glory in the rest.
But none perceived, so dazzled as we were,
That Bird, and Horse, and Man were gone.
Only the Lady stayed.

'I say that they were gone, or seen no more,
But left their light amongst us, though it faded
Then, as the sun fades from a wall,
From all except from her. And so shone ever
However fitfully in us
Most steadfastly in her.
We had seen its differing brightness
In modes of wonder, thought and loving-kindness,
And as light differs in wick, in wire, in planet,
So variously it gave
Its brilliance to our love.'

A Matter of Life and Death

I did not see the iris move,
I did not feel the unfurling of my love.

This was the sequence of the flower:
First the leaf from which the bud would swell,
No prison, but a cell,
A rolled rainbow;
Then the sheath that enclosed the blow
Pale and close
Giving no hint of the blaze within,
A tender skin with violet vein.
Then the first unfurling petal
As if a hand that held a jewel
Curled back a finger, let the light wink
Narrowly through the chink,
Or like the rays before the sunrise
Promising glory.

And while my back is turned, the flower has blown.
Impossible to tell
How this opulent blossom from that spick bud has grown.
The chrysalis curled tight,
The flower poised for flight –
Corolla with lolling porphyry wings
And yellow tiger markings
A chasing-place for shade and light:
Between these two, the explosion
Soundless, with no duration.
        (I did not see the iris move,
        I did not feel my love unfurl.)
The most tremendous change takes place in silence,
Unseen, however you mark the sequence,
Unheard, whatever the din of exploding stars.

Down the porphyry stair
Headlong into the air
The boy has come: he crouches there
A tender startled creature
With a fawn's ears and hair-spring poise
Alert to every danger
Aghast at every noise.
A blue blink
From under squeezed-up lids
As mauve as iris buds
Is gone as quickly as a bird's bright wink.
Gone – but as if his soul had looked an instant through the chink.
And perfect as his shell-like nails,
Close as are to the flower its petals,
My love unfolded with him.
Yet till this moment what was he to me?
Conjecture and analogy;
Conceived, and yet unknown;
Behind this narrow barrier of bone
Distant as any foreign land could be.

I have seen the light of day,
Was it sight or taste or smell?
What I have been, who can tell?
What I shall be, who can say?

He floats in life as a lily in the pool
Free and yet rooted;
And strong though seeming frail,
Like the ghost fritillary
That trails its first-appearing bud
As though too weak to raise it from the mud,
But is stronger than you dream,
And soon will lift its paper lantern
High upon an arched and sinewy stem.

His smiles are all largesse,
Need ask for no return,
Since give and take are meaningless
To one who gives by needing
And takes our love for granted
And grants a favour even by his greed.
The ballet of his twirling hands
His chirping and his loving sounds,
Perpetual expectation
Perpetual surprise –
Not a lifetime satisfies
For watching, every thing he does
We wish him to do always.

> *Only in a lover's eyes*
> *Shall I be so approved again;*
> *Only the other side of pain*
> *Can truth again be all I speak,*
> *Or I again possess*
> *A saint's hilarious carelessness.*

He rows about his ocean
With its leaning cliffs and towers,
A horizontal being,
Straddled by walking people
By table-legs and chairs;
And sees the world as you can see
Upside-down in water
The wavering heights of trees
Whose roots hang from your eyes.
Then Time begins to trail
In vanishing smoke behind him,

A vertical creature now
With a pocket full of nails,
One of a gang of urchin boys
Who proves his sex by robber noise –
Roar of the sucking dove
And thunder of the wren.
Terror waits in the woods
But in the sun he is brazen
Because our love is his
No matter what he does;
His very weakness claims a share
In the larger strength of others,
And perfect in our eyes
He is only vulnerable there.

But not immortal there, alas.
We cannot keep, and see. The shapes of clouds
Which alter as we gaze
Are not more transient than these living forms
Which we so long to hold
For ever in the moment's mould.
The figures frozen in the camera's record
And carried with us from the past
Are like those objects buried with the dead –
Temporal treasures irrelevant to their need.
Yes, this is the worst:
The living truth is lost,
And is supplanted by these album smiles.

> *What you desire to keep, you slay:*
> *While you watch me, I am going.*
> *Wiser than you, I would not stay*
> *Even if I could: my hope's in growing.*
> *My form as a dapple of sun that flies*
> *On the brook, is changed; my earliest word*
> *Is the call you learnt to recognize*
> *And now forget, of a strange bird.*

Yet, as the calyx contains the life of the bud
So the bud is contained within the flower
Though past in time:
The end is not more true than the beginning,

Nor is the promise cancelled by the prime.
Not only what he was, and is, but what he might have been,
In each is rolled within.
Our life depends on that:
What other claim have we to resurrection?
For now that we can contemplate perfection
We have lost the knack of being it. What should be saved
Of these distorted lives?
All we can pray is
                    Save us from Nothingness.
Nothingness, which all men dread;
Which makes us feel an irrational pity for the dead,
And fight the anodyne
Even while we long for deliverance from pain.

So, I have read,
When a man gave his darling in grief to the grave
About her neck in a locket tied
He set this urgent word –
Not to drink Lethe, at all costs not to forget.
And this is truth to us, even yet.
For if life is eternal
All must be held, though all must be redeemed.
But what can ever restore
To these sad and short-coming lives of ours
The lovely jocund creatures that we were
And did not know we were?
What can give us at once
The being and the sense?

Why, each within.
Has kept his secret for some Resurrection:
The wonder that he was
And can be, which is his
Not by merit, only by grace.
It comes to light, as love is born with a child,
Neither with help nor herald
(I did not see the iris move);
Neither by sight nor sound –
I did not feel the unfurling of my love.

The Images that Hurt...

'The images that hurt and that connect'
W.H. Auden

All the materials of a poem
Are lying scattered about, as in this garden
The lovely lumber of Spring.
All is profusion, confusion: hundred-eyed
The primulae in crimson pink and purple,
Golden at the pupil;
Prodigal the nectarine and plum
That fret their petals against a rosy wall.
Flame of the tulip, fume of the blue anemone,
White Alps of blossom in the giant pear-tree,
Peaks and glaciers, rise from the same drab soil.

Far too much joy for comfort:
The images hurt because they won't connect.
No poem, no possession, therefore pain.
And struggling now to use
These images that bud from the bed of my mind
I grope about for a form,
As much in the dark, this white and dazzling day,
As the bulb at midwinter; as filled with longing
Even in this green garden
As those who gaze from the cliff at the depths of sea
And know they cannot possess it, being of the shore
And severed from that element for ever.

Portholland and Greeb Point

For A.W.

The fourth wall no scale can measure:
    The fourth wall is the sea.
Sometimes it is close, enormous, glassy,
    Sometimes rolled away,
Sometimes troubled and towering comes
    Into the room to impart the storm.
We sit – or swim – the sense is doubtful where
    We in the sea's life share.

In the pool's depth the cloud's reflection
    Quakes like curds in a bowl;
And at my breath the surface shudders
    Then again is still
As when the lighthouse flashing breaks
    And then restores the dark.
So clear, the minnows seem to swim in air
    And in the sky's life share.

The sticklebacked and brackeny headland
    Nosing in the bay
Is where I ruled an impregnable castle
    In my minnow day:
I am gazing into the pool, and watch
    That minnow life, but cannot reach it;
Through years like water I watch, so near, so clear,
    A life I cannot share.

St Ishmael's

This valley waits. For whom is it waiting?
This valley is holding its breath. Till when?

Not far off, the gnashing sea,
Gobbled rock and wind-lashed headland;
Here, a calm viridian valley,
Sap and silence.

Down in the deep wood stand the fruit-trees
Laden with apples. Who will pick them?
Thick wood crowds against the wall,
Within the wall is woodland crowding
Outwards: where is the house, the garden?
Gone. Where is the wonder who
Should make his entrance? Not yet come.

The valley is waiting. Not for us.

No one stirs, not a bird; only
An idiot down in the cove jabbers
And fights his shadow: cocks a snook,
With Peep Bo behind the wall.
His part's designed: the Anti-Masque
To a solemn drama – mocks the hero
Still awaited.-Rusty rocks
That dip in a level estuary sea
Hundreds of million years have waited.

Part the bamboo thicket: there
Is the grey chapel you thought to find,
Eyebrow-deep in rhododendrons,
Dittany-of-Crete with dangling crimson,
Flaring pokers, pallid fuchsia.

The valley is waiting.

So our lives wait for the blaze of glory
Always expected. Each with a secret,
Cluttered with leaves, with flowers and fruit,
Silence caught by the sleeve, to stay
Till the new glory enters the scene.
But when, or how, is out of sight;
Or whether it is for death we wait,
And his the called-for, marvellous entrance.

Making Love, Killing Time

The clock within us, speaking time
By heart-beat seconds and by mental years,
Is garrulous in any gear,
So life at once seems short and endless.
Who is not glad to find the hour later than he thought?
For so he has killed, not time
But the inward timing of the ceaseless rote.
Its beat, which makes him count the cost
Of that creation which, loving, he cannot resist,
Hurries him on to end whatever was begun –
The child, to be grown, the poem, to be done.

But in each other's arms,
Or on the tide of prayer, when we
Encountering souls support each other, like swimmers in a
    blissful sea,
The cost is known as the cause of bliss,
And the gabbling rote is heard as a murmur of peace.
So *making love* we say, but love makes us
Again to be as in our listening-time,
When, hearing our heart-beat, we took it for the world's,
And with no wish to escape it, then and there
Loved what we were.

Choosing a Name

My little son, I have cast you out
    To hang heels upward, wailing over a world
    With walls too wide.
My faith till now, and now my love:
    No walls too wide for that to fill, no depth
    Too great for all you hide.

I love, not knowing what I love,
    I give, though ignorant for whom
    The history and power of a name.
I conjure with it, like a novice
    Summoning unknown spirits: answering me
    You take the word, and tame it.

Even as the gift of life
    You take the famous name you did not choose
    And make it new.
You and the name exchange a power:
    Its history is changed, becoming yours,
    And yours by this: who calls this, calls you.

Strong vessel of peace, and plenty promised,
    Into whose unsounded depths I pour
    This alien power;

Frail vessel, launched with a shawl for sail,
  Whose guiding spirit keeps his needle-quivering
  Poise between trust and terror,

And stares amazed to find himself alive;
  This is the means by which you say *I am*,
  Not to be lost till all is lost,
When at the sight of God you say *I am nothing*,
  And find, forgetting name and speech at last,
  A home not mine, dear outcast.

The Gaze

Your light is not yet broken:
Single the seven colours stream
In one white eyebeam from your self to mine.
My look, refracted and coloured by desires
Brings home a half-truth, but when you look at me
It is as though you had thrown a line
Out from your cradle to draw my image back.
Mirrors return the image which we show them,
But like a thinker, when you reflect on me
You take me in. And this without deceit,
Since you are open and since looks are free.

God is the source on which you should gaze like that.
I am not worth it; looking at me, you must learn
Selection, and suppress some part of the truth,
For art or kindness' sake. But not for love's.
For love (which has no need to blame or praise)
Waken that white beam again, reminding me
That I was born for this, to watch my Maker
Ever, with such a humble, thirsty gaze.

Nothing is Lost

Nothing is lost.
We are too sad to know that, or too blind;
Only in visited moments do we understand:
It is not that the dead return –
They are about us always, though unguessed.

This pencilled Latin verse
You dying wrote me, ten years past and more,
Brings you as much alive to me as the self you wrote it for,
Dear father, as I read your words
With no word but Alas.

Lines in a letter, lines in a face
Are faithful currents of life: the boy has written
His parents across his forehead, and as we burn
Our bodies up each seven years,
His own past self has left no plainer trace.

Nothing dies.
The cells pass on their secrets, we betray them
Unknowingly: in a freckle, in the way
We walk, recall some ancestor,
And Adam in the colour of our eyes.

Yes, on the face of the new born,
Before the soul has taken full possession,
There pass, as over a screen, in succession
The images of other beings:
Face after face looks out, and then is gone.

Nothing is lost, for all in love survive.
I lay my cheek against his sleeping limbs
To feel if he is warm, and touch in him
Those children whom no shawl could warm,
No arms, no grief, no longing could revive.

Thus what we see, or know,
Is only a tiny portion, at the best,
Of the life in which we share; an iceberg's crest
Our sunlit present, our partial sense,
With deep supporting multitudes below.

The Freezing Rose

All wear the freezing rose
This winter season,
Like the flesh we carry
A common agony
The ground of joys and sorrows.

When all are covered so in glory
Who is to be proud
Who is to be bowed in shame?
Snow upon the roof-tree
Snow upon the leafing tree.

The shade covered with sapphire;
With white sleep the nursling:
His sappy fingers,
And withered kex of working hands,
As the sun descends,
With the same reflected fire.

'With my body I thee worship.'
This is to dispense with
Distrust of the sense
And of one's own ugliness:
The new-born, the warped and worn,
Beauty, suffering, splendour,
Bear this common shape.

And to love those
Is love without longing.
I make offering
Of what each one possesses –
The common, fallen rose.

Before the Fall

Yes, the most excellent beauties come unearned,
    I think as I look at you:
But quite unpaintable, unprintable, and alas
    Unmemorable too.
That face which the camera fixes on a sheet,
    That smiling daisy face,
Becomes a changeling that memory rocks in the cradle
    In the living child's place.
The look of a foreign child, the smell of a bonfire,
    Will come to mind at a call,
But not you, sand-hopper, builder of falling towers,
    Whose beauty seems eternal.

We shall know too many of you as time goes on
    To keep one image clear.
A stranger would paint first the aureole
    Of hay-and-spun-glass hair,
And then, coming to the imp's eyes, might pause...
    But still for a little while
Glory and mischief agree together, and
    To cross the social will
Is a good joke, since nothing wholly divides
    You from the milk you spilt,
And so, having no sense of separation
    You have no sense of guilt.

To glory in mischief – this is the happiness to which
    The lunatic and criminal aspire,
Remembering that they were once adorable
    In all they did, and felt the impartial fire.
But you, urchin, hérichon, with prickles
    Of temper and restless trotting feet,
Can do outrageous things unblamed, because
    Your gazing self is lost
In what it contemplates, like the seraphim that know –
    The cherubim that love – most.

Two Commissioned Pieces

1. A CAROL TO BE SET TO MUSIC

commissioned by Thomas Armstrong

Young beam of heaven, enclosed within
The lantern of a human form,
How shall we face the full-blown light
Who find the bud too sharp for sight?

All brilliance known to human eyes –
White light of winter-burning skies,
Gold light that gives the green its glow
And makes a rose of sullen snow –

All these, the blessed lights of earth
Are little candles to his birth:
Too bright to bear, but that he could
Find means to make our weakness good.

Our darkness gives his light its place,
Our darkness gives a Prince his peace:
He puts his life within our hands,
And in that cradle sleeps, and shines.

2. STONE ANGEL

For a photograph of the font at Taynton

I had a beginning but shall have no end:
Even though the blade
Of razing Time
Abrades my form, and though I fade
From memory, stranger, even then
Blazing creatures of my kind
Will cry, 'Glory to God and peace to men.'

Bathing off Roseland

The sea, that turns old bottles into gems,
  Has made of me a bird.
  Now with all four wings outspread
I dip and hover, vacillate recover
    Lulled and directionless,
  Who on the cliff with conscious tread
  Moved to some purpose.

It is a firmament that curves below,
  Colour of capsicum green
  And purple bloom of aubergine;
Wayward and flippant I am in my element,
    Feeling the speed
  Of the wheeling world and the sails careening
  Above my head.

I am sustained by powers not my own,
  As on the tide of prayer
  Another's love can sway me toward
Some good that of myself I would not:
    Powerful, hidden to me,
  As the purpose which drives these great ships forward
  Parting the sea.

Leaving Ringshall

A quodlibet of voices in one self

  O constant moon
  You shine for ever on that terrace, where
  The sweetbriar smells are rinsed through air
  Of after-the-shower.
  The height of summer and the moon on duty:
  Roses waterfalling to the lawn,
  Their daytime rainbow vanished, giving place
  To the single-shining, pungent-seeming rays.

There the young self
In painful soundless yammer to the night
Makes prayer for sensual delight,
And peace, and power to speak;
While an articulate music from the house
Speaks for it, flowing to cliffs of beech,
That like an unattainable longed-for Hebrides
Raise darker shapes upon dark bracken seas.

Yes, the inconstant moon is constant there
And ever shines; the waterfall of roses
Dropping over the bank drops never a petal.
But in what place, and in what time?
Has my passion the power to force all others
To share my moment and my point of sight?
I cannot have left my image on that terrace:
I did no murder there, suffered no violence
From any exterior power;
Love without violence does not leave a ghost.
So I suppose I shall not haunt the newcomers:
And yet the place haunts me –
                    which haunts the other?
I cannot see it empty of myself
As in contemplation of a person
I can forget my gazing eyes.
Because a place is loved for what we felt there,
Not for itself alone. Yet in a portrait
The setting holds the key: met out of context
A face is nameless, or if daily seen,
Confused in memory by its many frames.

So, though we treat the landscape as a background,
Without it we are – nowhere.
                    Each to his haunt:
Though I appear in yours and you in mine
It is not in our common time or space,
But in that sad dimension of the mind
Where ghosts have senses, meet, and yet are alone,
Vivid and inaccessible.
                    How I look for you
Ghosts of my house . . . My father comes to meet me
Hearing the sound of my arriving wheels

And leaving logs balanced across the sawing-horse,
A gentle greeting figure, his bird-stained hat
Crowning his splendid forehead – here I have him:
Broken nose, sceptical mouth, and hands
Bramble-scarred of a scholar turned to grass;
The *Paradiso* on his lavatory shelf
That love should find each corner of his life,
As my mother fills his house with gaiety and snapdragon....
Family life, that filled it at a spring tide,
Ebbing has left a wrack of letters, fiddles,
Diaries, dumb-bells and domestic playbills,
Croquet-hoops and solitaire and stilts –
A peaceful littered shore from which we gaze
Where the tide of wheat still rushes over the meadow,
The solid sea of clay beneath us breaks
In russets and raspberries, cherry, thyme and cistus,
And the sweet briar, whose scent has flown me here.

> Who lives in the house?
> The family gave no vacant possession
> For what can dispossess a passion?

> Space is no absolute prison:
> You need not change with a dead person
> Like Monte Cristo, flung to an ocean

> Of fearful new sensation
> To struggle, a stone tied to your feet –
> It is an instant easy flight

> Upon a plane of thought
> A beckon of scent, to a well-known place,
> So here we are, crowding the house.

> Although we had closed its eyes
> And tried to acquire the knack of parting,
> Turning away for a fresh start.

> How can we learn to part?
> And which of us deserts the other –
> We who move
> Or the house which stays, for a new owner?

So, if I had the power to turn you back to the self you think of so,
Back to that moon-gazing girl of twenty years ago,
You would thank me? You would joyfully take the chance? Indeed, no.
Not only because of the queasy pains of youth, when an unwilling
    change
Is forced on us by each new meeting, every charming stranger,
Until we cannot tell *who* we are, and waste our strength in
   rearranging
Faces in the mirror. (Unless to love we make them over,
And by that testament discover who indeed we are.)

But when so much is lost with youth, why should I reject your
    offer?
What is the obstinate instinct that still wishes to move?
All things flow, said the Greek, and I suppose we partly love
What we must do, though something in us is crying for loss, and
    disapproves.
Crying for loss of the adored master Virgil, for loss of the tender
    friend –
How bleak and dull the way to walk without them to the end.
Yes, an irretrievable loss. And yet we rejoice to find
The finishing touch; the end of the story. Which would be absurd
Unless – unless for a deeper reason: that at last we dared
To remember the look of God. For as a child bereft, too strongly
    stirred
By memory of its parents' kindness, tries to remember their
    rougher mood,
We in our separation dare not think of God as He is indeed.

But if we dared to remember what it was, that instant glance we
    had
From God, that looked away all loss –
And if, as a bee on a hidden beam, the heart were homing toward
    that place,
Pulling us forward, then no wonder we were glad to see time
    pass.

Time passed and good foregone, for the sake of some more
    difficult good
That draws us on its beam – the ineluctable love of God.

A Matter of Life and Death   131

On Changing Places

For two musicians

And is there such a word as parting?
Reason affirms it, but the heart
Denies, and risks a deal of pain
By debts of joy received and given;
While time spins on like a spider, weaves
With years for thread, with hour and season,
Twisting the figure of daily lives,
And warps it fast to the place it loves.

Music must come to its final cadence
When its angel falls to silence:
The sound renews, but yet his voice
Can never speak the same word twice.

The heart, so soundly given the lie,
Is yet most constant to believe
That what is good can never die.
The substitute does not deceive
But comes to be loved for its own sake:
As in London tree and lake
Embed the country in the town,
The yaffle sounds with the motor horn,
The white sails flash, and the earth smells;
And in this city-pastoral
Exiles can see rare beauties, mark
The brilliant green on soot-black bark.

Now that you are changing place,
And music in this mode must cease,
May it not die, but hold its peace!
And may such peace hold you. For now
Blossoms from a fruiting bough
Must spring, as on the orange tree
Beside the golden globes of fruit
Promising, glistening flowers shoot.

Mountain Shrine near Lerici

Rose of the rocks that loves the mountain dryness
Grows here tall as a garden rose,
Tiny broom creeps in the grass with many strange-flowered orchis,
And here, on the dry-sweet mountain plain
Is set the shrine.
Ilex encircle it, their plated leaves
Like armour greaves,
And the cool bead curtains of the olives
Are hung against the hot blue sky.
'Welcome,' once was written over the doorway,
'Welcome to men and to all spirits.'
A dangerous invitation, long since cancelled.
And yet, if such a welcome could be spoken anywhere
It surely would be here.
The mountains embrace the sea, an alien creed,
The sea bears up the swimmer's head,
And Venus, rising from a turquoise wave
On to white rocks, bequeaths her shrine to Peter.
Flowers rush to the all-distinguishing light,
Each form defined – the open-handed fig-tree,
Arbutus with its emery fruit,
Hermit juniper, each in its proud identity;
And human life spills out of doors –
All is in sight
In the oecumenical light.

O elsewhere, or at other seasons,
Evil spirits menace through the fog,
And we must wall us in and ward off terrors;
The dancing lights will lead us to a bog,
Despair can drown us, even in buoyant waters,
Squalls arise, and the poet sinks like a stone.
But here is the shrine which said
'Everything that lives is good';
And now the dancing spirits are seen
As when the sky sheds diamonds down
That trouble the sea's surface like drops of rain;
Or when, at night,
The valley seems a sky beneath our feet
Where fireflies flash among the trees like stars.

Porto Venere

From the Italian of Eugenio Montale[1]

There, from waves lapping
The sills of a Christian temple,
There the Triton rises.
    Every coming hour
Has lived in the past, and
Every doubt is led by the hand
Like a friendly girl.

No self-regarding gaze is there,
Nor hearkening to self.
There, you are at the beginning,
To choose is unwise;
Later you will depart again
To assume disguise.

[1] Previously unpublished, but written at the time of the preceding poem.

Two Voices

> *'L'instant de la mort est . . . l'instant où pour une fraction infinitésimale du temps la vérité pure, nue, certaine, éternelle entre dans l'âme.'*
> SIMONE WEIL

You learn the feasts of love when they are past,
Discern a banquet through a fast.

Not the death-bed only, and the silence
Clouding over it, but moments lit with sun –
Parting over the gate before an audience
Of smiling flowers, or on Ludgate Hill
Where we were silent, only the traffic bellowed
For pain, hearing the sentence of farewell . . .

This too is the hour of death.

And as a wounded man whose hurt is mortal
Feels at first but little pain, or none,
The heart goes free at first perhaps, but later
Returning to the scene, time and again
Wakes its own anguish, would not wish its ending,
Trying to grasp the meaning by the pain.

Parting is death, and death ends love.

If that were true, why does the injured creature
Fly homing constantly to that one scene?
I have seen a sparrow, her nest moved by the thatcher,
Flutter for hours at the spot where it should have been,
Deaf to the chirps, blind to the beaks of her nestlings
Only a couple of feet away; and so
The heart flies to the past, and cannot enter.
What does it hope to achieve? Perhaps to improve
Its own performance in the past, to alter
Some gawky fact to a more endurable shape?
Some gesture of love or powerful word spoken
Instead of the stammer of history? That's not all,
That's not the inescapable need that beckons.

I was blind to my love, but when
He went from me, I saw him then.

The need that draws us back to the moment of death
Is this, then: that we know we sometime, somehow
Must make it good. That was the flash of truth,
Infrequent star just for that instant visible:
If there was anguish, that was not the point,
And to have missed the point was inexcusable.

I have forgotten the insight with the pain.

Did you see God in parting from Him? Learn
To make the moment bless you; haunt the scene;
For if the parting-point was the point of vision,
Then only through that gate can we return.

A Thrust through Time

'I was in Canaan when Absalom was slain...'

TALIESSIN

The dahlia deep in a dark cellar
  Waiting for light, looks dead, but is not:
  Points of green youth prick through the skin:
Charge of life in a toil-worn tuber.

Magnolia tree, plumed for flight
  Against earth's gravity; mother of pearl –
  How great a force thrust through the bark
With flowering fires toward the light!

How strong the life in these. And love
  That colours every physical thing
  With godlike joy; that makes adorable
Not only the lovely, but all that live –

Could not love thrust through time, as life
  Through these hard stems, a strain of joy
  To those whose anguish aches through time,
And take the strain of dumb-bell grief?

To stand with Cranmer in the fire,
  With Coleridge when his love destroyed him,
  Even to lift for a little his lifelong
Pain of unfulfilled desire.

Too late. Unless indeed that power
  Which raised in us the wish to assuage
  Did, then, through us a work of mercy –
Strength in the flame, joy for an hour.

Lyme Regis – Golden Cap

'For soul is form, and doth the body make.'
SPENSER

The Cobb curves like a fossil, ridged and gray.
That sickle hook, which once held navies in its crook,
Still shields the town, and reaps the golden stalks
That spring in the wave;
Cliffs are sliced about the bay
Like Gloucester cheese (and the sea a bowl of pale whey);
These, and even the fossil shells
Uncovered by the tide twice in a day,
Immortal in clay their grave and their preservative,
Shall all be worn away.
That idling sauntering sea which suddenly shows its teeth in a
    white snarl,
That yielding seeling sea which hardly lifts a finger,
Steadily swallows the cliffs of clay
(And the spirit wears the flesh away):
The trembling hawk, the trembling sea, hard on their prey.

Rocks at the cliff's foot seem dead souls
Bound in these boulder shapes, with headless
Torsoes, rounded thighs and shoulders,
Bodies that would not take the mould
Of spirit, as though
The flesh for ever were only flesh:
Prone upon a forlorn shore
Until as small shingle all
Under the grinding tide are rolled.
Baptized of water and the spirit,
But not as rocks to shingle, not as cliffs to sand
Would we endure our transformation:
To move as light through water, not to be lost like a drop in the
    sea –
The body with the soul's design
Firm as the ammonite's, but free,
And by its form, divine.

News of the World

1

Love is our argument of joy,
Its cadence is the tierce de picardy;
Early love is the rare, thin
May-day hymn
Sun-rising from the river tower.

And what are love's infallible signs?
A clutch of fear as someone enters;
Dumb darkness when he is gone;
But in between
The night-blowing Cereus breaks into flower

And all the constellations bless.
Such a calm and glow of glory
In his presence, that distress
Seems meaningless:
So gay, serene, supreme his power.

2

Meeting of mercy and truth –
A reconciling vision
That every man has known
Although he makes no sign,
Although we read no news
In eyes as dead as clinkers
Incapable now of fire.
How hard to imagine his figure –
Sedate on City stairway –
As Love's wild creature
Transported by desire
Or by the bliss of prayer.
Seeing his doldrum state
We search the *News of the World*
For the history of his heart
(Since those who miss the unbroken
Radar beam of sanctity
Have yet some sound of heaven –
All the kinds of passion

Even the spider love
That mates and then devours
Have been for an instant blessed);
Or we read the signs of a secret –
A rash on a girl's cheek,
A nervous twitch, or a stammer,
Index of an inward truth
Too fierce to be supported,
Too intricate to express.

3

Quitted but in your arms I lie:
Give and take are equal joy.
Is it to live like God, to want
And have at once? To have what's spent,
To nourish need because fulfilment
Cannot fail; postpone its coming,
Then with this voluntary need
Turn to will a world of good.

'Love is simply the willing of good.'
What I cried for, I had;
More than I knew I had, I gave.
To find the reason for my birth
I no more question – this is enough.
This is the place toward which I went,
Though to keep it but a moment,
Graced, and favoured, and content.

4

'Lost, lost, it is lost!'
His name cried out in the heart
Each moment – if the air
Made audible even a part
Of those wild noiseless cries
The sound would strike us deaf as stone.

They make no sign, but perish.
We do not know what desolation
Hollows behind the deadpan face

And casual conversation.
The fowl still runs upright
Although its neck is broken.

Is he dead, or afar,
Did he lóve léss than yóu did?
Why do you smile, dress, order
Dinner, if he is dead?
A calm, visible action,
A horrible clamour within.

'Shall I ever find again
My heart of exchanging fire?
Or will it lie for ever
Fused in despair?
After the deadlock of pain
The give and take of life again?'

5

Love is our interest, love our capital theme.
A fortune all may have who wish
And none can lose unless they wish.
We are bankrupt, not through death,
Not through joy's cessation,
Not for any privation,
But ceasing to wish for good.
We who have wished a little good
And have received much,
Long to endow the world, to expend
Something of that free splendour
(Happiness flowers in bounty).
And yet before fulfilment
Too often the desire is spent,
And by the morning light
Ecstasy seems another planet;
So into destitution
We fall who sometime lived in the lap of glory.
Yet there the world belongs,
There the world is secured,
Hidden in light, if we could look.
As when the rays of the sun

Through a wall of alabaster
Glow in unfocused amber,
The light itself is plain
Though the source is unseen,
We see the selfless rejoicing
Of lives spent bringing to birth
Children of other women,
The humble eye for fact
Of poets, a great man's innocence,
His dowser's touch for truth...

These speak to us: if all could speak
Then we might learn from all men
Their true news of love:
Of love, the organ of life,
The manual of perfection,
Absolute lord, adored.

Cranmer and the Bread of Heaven

'...the bread had nothing to do with the Body – that was what
he was dying for –'
DOM GREGORY DIX on Cranmer

Dear master, was it really for this you died?
    To make that separation clear
    That heaven is elsewhere, nowise here?
That the divine bitter yeast is not inside
    Our common bread; this body, loved so
In its young crocus light, and the full orb of manhood,
    And the paean of sound, all that our senses know
Is not the matter of God?

The 'last enchantments of the Middle Age'
    In this case, were a faggot fire
    And rubbish pitched beside the pyre;
A couple of burnt doors, from this so-intellectual rage
    Remain, and the proposition (if dying made it plain)
Flesh turns to ashes, bread cannot turn to God.
    Yet how if the question that cost so much pain
Itself was wrongly made?

A change takes place: to this all can assent;
   But question 'what place does it take?
   Or none at all?' – there's the mistake,
There we confuse our terms. For this is an event,
   Not subject to a physical experiment
As water is split for energy; no gain
   In splitting hairs. We know that God can enter
To what He first contained;

We know the kingdom of heaven suffers violence,
   But not atomic. Who can weigh
   Love in a man's heart? So we still say
'Body and soul' as though they were at variance.
   Who can weigh Love? Yet sensibly he burns,
His conflagration is eyes, hands, hearts:
   So is he sensed, but in and out of the eternal,
Because the sense departs.

Anniversary

This fig-tree spreads all hands toward the light,
   Five broad fingers to each, solid and still
   As those that are chiselled on pulpit or stall.
And yet the light pervades those carven leaves,
Not as my dark hands divert the sun
   If I hold them before my face –
   These invert it, let it pass,
A green effulgence that the trunk receives.

These fifteen years I have spread my hands to the light of your
      love.
Its rays should long ago have made me strong:
   Did my remorse for wrong
Or fears filter its power from the light,
Or did my darkness divert it from my heart,
   That I am still so callow and unsure,
   And cannot think to endure
Even the shortest winter out of your sight?

Evenlode

A fable of rivers
Designed for broadcasting
with music

Characters

Narrator
Boy
Alpheus
Arethusa

NARRATOR (*speaking while music plays*)
Drops of music, or water.
We speak of a fountain playing: this one sings.
You hear it: will you see it also?
Listeners, spectators, who surround me,
Your hidden eyes like stars too far to be seen.
I speak to you as one beside a jungle fire,
Talking to those beyond the limit of light.
Have they horns, tusks, or human faces?
He only guesses, but in his fable
Shares with them sight and sound.

Drops of music, or water;
Tongue of a girl or a spring.
Three tones of the oleander,
Clash of cistus, hibiscus,
Sharps and flats of rock on ripple,
Jangle of bubbles to the surface.
This is the fountain's voice,
Voice of Arthusa,
Once a girl, now a spring,
At peace here
Past fear,
Also – past hope.

Arethusa, a virgin vowed
To Artemis and chastity,
Who fled from a river-god, Alpheus, over
Burning hills and under heavy seas,
And rose again in Sicily

As a perpetual spring.
Imprisoned in her shape of water
She has lost for ever
The prize she would preserve;
Losing her form of a girl,
Receiving the form of the god,
Exactly as if she had stayed
To suffer the invasion of his river nature.

Drops of music, or water.
Not the springs of Sicily now
But the green streams of England.
From the train you see, but cannot hear them;
In the train, passing by, it is safe to desire them.

The train and the river move over the map,
Meeting and parting as partners who set to each other
And make their chain in a country dance.
But the train is a stranger, a restless spectator
Always, while the river, wherever it flows,
Is part of the scene, and the mud that forms its bed
Is the limestone slopes, the golden walls of the houses,
And the green leaves it has swallowed and digested.
Fetch out of your mind those heavy afternoons
When you were dozing in your carriage corner,
After a starchy knapsack-lunch,
And let the landscape, like a ticker-tape,
Flicker across your eyeballs.
We cross and cross the river, that seems to curl
As a pliable vine about the rigid railway line,
And suddenly, at a bend, is the white house
That looks all day at its image in the stream.
Its windows waver as the water wavers,
The ripples wrinkle its brows;
Its porch is a rainbow, duckweed its green creeper,
And chinking lawns, cool chives and lettuce
Are fed by the river.

You know the place? Children sit on the banks
With primrose laps, and make their springy bunches,
Then pelt the waterfall with flowers.
The owner stands on a bridge and smokes his pipe,

Gazing like his house down at the current.
Why doesn't he dive in the stream?
Is the sight too dear to be possessed,
And does his peaceful pose conceal
A doubtful longing, as my napping figure
Propped in the carriage corner?
Perpetual watchers, both of us,
Only in thought immersed?

But this is the place of peace and unending happiness:
Every day a summer Sunday,
The daily chores as wished-for as a cadence,
No grease in the bowl, no pests in the garden,
No boredom at the insipid noon, or despair
At the ineluctable dawn.
And what are we to this? Strangers,
Glassed away and passing on,
Muffled in foolish garments, passing on,
Losing even the sight of it.

If you remember the place, you will understand.
You will have wanted, as I did, to belong there,
To leave the train, the wandering eye,
To fix the vision, plunge in the river.
The map discovered the spot: my glance explored
The green windings of the stream
Between the contour lines and stripes of buff,
The cherry-weather names – Charlbury, Combe,
Wilcote, Stonesfield, Shipton-under-Wychwood.
And while my eyes explored the symbols
My ears were filled with the river-god's song –
The river Evenlode, or any other.
So the god sang to me, out of the map.

THE RIVER-GOD, ALPHEUS

My eyes are white stones
That shine through water
As the moon
Through a glistening mist.
My limbs the supple ripples
That part like a fan

A Matter of Life and Death   145

Or fuse into one,
Wrinkle and fade
As lines erased
On a carbon pad.
The racing weed
Is my green hair.
Stare in the pool
My wraith is there
In a wreath of water
Around a rock;
Look for long
It will disappear.
My name is Evenlode
Windrush or Dove;
Or else Alpheus
Ladon, Leucyanias.
Water as dark
As a night with glittering
Stars of the frogbit;
Water so clear
That the peering fish
Fear their own shadows;
As sleek as oil
Or boiling down
In white cascades
And braids of glass.
Choose my name
And paint my scene
After your choice
I am still the river.
You passers-by
Who share my journey,
You move and change,
I move but am the same;
We travel together
You moving trains,
You move and are gone,
I move and remain.

NARRATOR

It was April, the day I saw it first,
With a June warmth, but only skin deep.
Blackthorn bushes beside the footbridge
Scattered confetti in the pool, as if
To mark the wedding of winter and summer.
Now as I come on foot, those nuptials
Are long past, and the time of fruiting grass
And silent air is come. Instead of the blackthorn
The papery burnet rose dips in the stream;
Those wholesome summer girls
Angelica, Sweet Cicely,
Rooted cool in the juicy mud,
Heads hot in the sun,
Stand by an army of teasels, still half-armed and green.

There is the house, under its mothering slope:
The house is waiting for me,
I am coming into the picture,
I am crossing the bridge – I am nearly there –
Silent air, yes, except for a wren
Far up in the woods, whose song begins
Gently like a wheel at the top of a hill
And quickens to helter-skelter:
And so my heart.

The bridge is behind me,
I have stepped into the picture,
But the place is deserted – no primrose children,
No contemplative smoker.
Not for me the house was waiting;
I have arrived, a stranger.

O bitter, bitter,
To make the pilgrimage, and reach the place,
And find oneself a stranger.
It is not quite deserted: a boy is running down:
Not one of the primrose children – a ragamuffin
All tufts and dungarees. He's going to bathe:
Bother the boy – what right has he to come here?

BOY

For some, the sea:
To battle and vault
Over the sleazy waves with cocky crests,
The cut and slash of salt;
But for me
On the alkaline river, the mild and ale-brown river
To rock and rest
In the shallows and hear the hiss of the sallows is best.

NARRATOR

Now, I see the urchin does belong here.
As soon as he touched the water, he was transformed.
His cockatoo head with its wiry crest of hair
Is as fit for the stream as a bulrush.
His limbs melt into lilies,
He is free of the water;
The reeds, the moorhen's nest, the ooze and bubble
Are all his home.

BOY

The yammering trees
Must speak for the wind,
And so on the noisy hill the word goes by
With a waterfall sound;
But below, at peace,
Is the havering river, the devious dawdling river
Where now I lie
And floating follow the lazy yachts of the sky.

NARRATOR

He does belong – and I? –
O bitter, bitter,
To make the pilgrimage, and reach the place,
And find oneself a stranger.

BOY

Come on in, it's smashing.
Not cold, but cool as lemon squash.

These yellow lilies smell like brandy.
I'll show you a moorhen's nest – it's got five eggs:
That means she hasn't finished yet; they go
To ten or eleven. Come on in, it's lovely.

NARRATOR

Shall I? It can't be as lovely as it looks.
And if I jump, I lose the look.
Whatever I do, a stranger...

BOY

What are you saying?

NARRATOR

I am wondering whether to bathe.

BOY

Come on, come on, it's lovely.
I'm floating along with the current: I'm lying on a cloud
Watching the trees and the sky – I'm flying through them –
A cool cloud or a pearl. Come on, it's lovely.

NARRATOR

Shall I? I can't see you now.
I've looked so long into the streaming weed
That now I see a face there. It's not yours, boy.
Is it a face, or formed of fuming stones
And waving light, with green weed for hair?
It melts, and then again is there.
Spirit, water, or flesh?

ALPHEUS

Arethusa!

NARRATOR

Echoes of sound – a man's voice;
Echoes of sight – a man's form in the stream;
And I am an echo of what I was.
The river god is calling out to his love,
And I am melting, fading;
I am here on the bank, I feel the earth beneath me;
And I am Alpheus, sleeping under the waters;
I am Arethusa, melting into the water...
The river god is speaking...

*

ALPHEUS
                       Arethusa!
It is I, Alpheus. Why did you run away from me?
You woke me, where I curled deep in my pool
Away from the scorching noon.
The light slipped down to me, through the crystal filter,
The light, stripped of its coarse hot pollen,
As cool and fine as a moonbeam,
And lapped me gently in my bed of sand.
In my sleep you came to me:
You danced like a dolphin in my pool,
Your skin was flushed with the pollen of light
And your hair burned like copper.
                    But in my stream
The golden limbs became pale silver,
And burnished hair, cooled and tarnished by water,
The green of rain-worn copper. I rose from my deeps,
Still half asleep I called your name,
And stretching up my arms I leapt to the surface,
Ready to seize those limbs
Which the waters already embraced.
But O, that peaceful trust I sleeping had,
Waking destroyed. Why did you run away from me?
Better to have lain with me in my plashy bed
Than struggle over the rocks and hills
That pitiless day.

ARETHUSA

On the firestone hills
Water flickers ahead,
And into air returning.
Black pools on the road
That fade as I approach them;
Water locked in a diamond
That mocks my thirst.

ALPHEUS

My waters were no mirage.
My shade was welcome after the savage hills.

ARETHUSA

Yes, after the glare of the sun
How gentle the freckled light upon your pool
How soft, after the flinty hillside
Your sandy shoal,
After the noise and sweat of hunting
How calm to swim, and cool.

ALPHEUS

Then why did you not stay?
I was no sun, to shrivel you up:
You would have melted into my embrace
And hardly known it: your limbs were almost water –
Cool water – already.

ARETHUSA

That was why.

ALPHEUS

Why?

ARETHUSA

        Because I half desired it
The sun would only have filled me with disgust:

To run from you was harder, therefore I must,
Or lose myself; break my trust.

ALPHEUS

You fled, but lost.
Since, in spite of all, you are what I am:
No longer a huntress, follower of Artemis,
But a spring of water.

ARETHUSA

As the twanging echoes of your voice came quivering upwards
I sprang to the shore.
The roots of your twining lilies held me back:
How useless it was to resist!
Although I reached the land, I ran from you
As one who treads in water against a current.
Naked I seemed to be wound with heavy clothing;
The air pressed me back:
The more I ran, the more I seemed immovable,
And your fingers, greedy like the foam fingers
That rush to grasp the rocks, were reaching after me.
The hill was laughing, innocent and green,
Oblivious of my pain:
It did not fear your shadow that outstripped me.
The dolphin-flowers were poised for flight:
I begged for speed from them – they would not hear me;
The chaste-tree, the friend of virgins,
Flaunted its purple petals, would not help me;
But then the love-in-a-mist, caerulean eyes
Behind a haze of tears, had pity
Showed me what I must do.
I called to Artemis, and as I called
The mist came down.

ALPHEUS

Yes, you were gone:
My hand closed on a cloud,
The light cloud escaped
My heavy shape of water.

ARETHUSA

You watched like a wild beast outside my hiding-place.
I heard your river voice, changed by your lust
To the salt-water howl of the sea,
And my fears chilled my mist to water.
Then you would have found me and possessed me,
But Artemis made me a passage under the earth,
And I lost the sun and the friendly sweet air
In a terror of darkness, which I still endure,
Though I spring to the light perpetually:
My fountain both my refuge and my prison.

ALPHEUS

I dared to be drowned in earth: I a stream
Died to the light for you. I pursued you
Under the ocean bed to the distant island.
But you had renounced the shape I loved, lost it for ever.

ARETHUSA

And must have lost it, though you had gained your wish
Even at your first rising.
None can devour and keep.
I am no more Arethusa
But a soft wraith of water,
Changed by my own desire.
Lost, both of us lost,
As soon as I touched your waters
That sultry day.

ALPHEUS

    And yet, after the glare of the sun
    How gentle the freckled light upon my pool;
    How soft, after the flinty hillside,
    My sandy shoal;
    After the noise and sweat of hunting
    How calm to swim, and cool.

    You should have stayed with me
    And lost your name

A Matter of Life and Death 153

As I in the great Ionian sea
Am lost, yet the same.
And Ladon, Erymanthus,
Rivers that join my waters,
Lose their titles too
(And I have lost you).
The north wind and I
Had the same cradle,
Born in Mount Boreas
I too was in Arcadia,
For ever passing by
(Since rivers have no home),
By vulgar Megalopolis
And long-lived Olympia,
A river of Elis
Flowing to make the sea
As you should have made, lost and found yourself in me.

*

BOY

Why ever didn't you come? It's smashing.
If you lie on your back, the current takes you
Round the bend and into a gooseflesh pool
So cold it almost scalds you.
I've done it twice and struggled back again
While you've been staring down at the patch of weed
As though you had dropped your eyes in.

NARRATOR

                    So I had.
And I went farther with the stream than you:
Down from the mountains, through the fields and into the sea.
Don't look so surprised – I didn't bathe,
And now I don't desire to.
But keep your river – swim while you can.
When you grow up, you'll find yourself a stranger,
Sadly hankering, like me.

BOY
But the moorhen's nest – don't you want to see it?

NARRATOR
Bring me a piece of river-weed instead.

BOY
Easy. A handful – catch it.

NARRATOR
                    Thank you
I shall take it home and press and keep it,
For this was a piece of the beard of the god Alpheus.

O bathing boy who must grow! O all you others
(Hidden eyes like stars too far to be seen)
Inveterate spectators, be at peace
With this your hankering joy:
Even to look is to leap,
And a dry weed may become
The beard of a river god
Even for those who have lost their delight in swimming,
Even for those who are strangers to the stream.

Choruses from 'The Trial of Thomas Cranmer'

Prologue
*Enter Witness, who speaks sometimes as an eye-witness of the martyrdom,
sometimes as Chorus.*

So wrote this hostile witness. How could he foresee
That the courage of Cranmer's end would be remembered
Through *his* words? We still have that letter of his,
And he was watching, four hundred years ago,
When the Primate of all England walked through the rain
To this church, and stood by this pillar – you can see
The marks of the scaffold – and hid his face
To escape our staring eyes. Later he was burnt
In the town ditch, like other refuse.

This witness, whose part I shall play, would have spoken
For the prosecution, yet is called by the defence.
And I shall give you words, you other witnesses,
Whether you sorrow for love or for pity:
You best, who lack conviction; you gentle, who are put upon;
You lovers of peace, who see that in war
We are all of us losers, whom both sides abuse;
You to whom words are lances, and actions a blunt axe;
There is something of you all in Cranmer, our godfather
Tortured under our tourist feet.
Have you looked for the cross in the road near Balliol,
Or built before your mind's eye a prison in the Cornmarket?
Look a little closer: here is that prison;
Here is Lambeth palace, while the sword still hovers
And has not fallen.

After SCENE II
(Cranmer is in prison, awaiting trial)

WITNESS

Each time has its prison cells, and we who see clearly
The tyranny of theirs, our hands are not clean.
We cannot feel their terror of anarchy and chaos;
Rebellion to us seems the part of the righteous –
Not so to them, where all rule was precarious.
But – two years in prison, and then to face the test!

Faith in a cause, or the glow of injured innocence,
Or hatred of one's captors – all that feeds courage,
Would have died in me, I am sure, before the end.
As the summer descended into winter, and rose
Once more to a roseless summer in a cell,
I should look out on the world with the eyes
Of the couldn't-care-less girl behind the counter:
Careless eyes, that see nothing worth the trouble
Of looking at, much less the trouble of dying.

O prisoners all, of all places and all times!
Frozen in the labour camp; warm in the bitter boredom
Of Wormwood Scrubbs; kings kept in the filth
Of castle dungeons; the innocent kept sleepless
In communist question-rooms – what tough goodness
Can survive untouched?
Prisoners are base, all but the very few,
The heroes, and I – I should not be one of them.

During SCENE IV

CRANMER (*who has yielded to persuasion, and promised to sign a recantation*)
What have I done? O, to sleep, and forget it all! (*He sleeps*)

WITNESS

If you could! But sleep is no death:
A fruitful waste of time that is crossed in – no time.
Where has the sleeper been? If he falls asleep
With a sentence on his lips, he will finish it on waking.
His time was his own, and fitted him as closely
As the blankets fit his body.

You tiny birds, that croodle from the cold
Under the bark of trees; beasts that fit the earth
To your forms; and men, that pull the universe
Snugly around you, your time is taken:
Wake, it is morning!

After SCENE IV

WITNESS

I cannot see it happen! I long to intervene,
To run before them, crying:
'You all believe in Christ, how can you so harm each other?
How will torture help the truth?' So much weary labour,
Such a faithful following of the kindly light
And mowing down others in your steadfast course!
As for us, the gentle ones, whose eyes are compound,
Whose eyes are like an insect's, and see on every side,
What have we done? Nothing but to suffer.
What has the Lord done? The Lord sits above!
So it ends, under a dismal rain, walking to the scaffold.

Then what remedy? I can see none:
I cannot reach into history a merciful finger
To turn back the torment. But could I face it there?
At the storm-centre of the truth, that torment?
Now, while he walks through weeping streets,
If I could have my wish, and step into history
As now I step upon the stage, what should I do?
Should I not act the part which now I play? *(Here he throws off his
        cloak, and reveals himself in sixteenth-century dress)*
Another mouth, to gape at his sufferings;
Another face uncaring; two more staring eyes.

EPILOGUE
(The Witness appears on top of the choir screen)

WITNESS

When they came to the stake – it was fixed at the place
Where Latimer and Ridley had suffered before him –
He knelt down and prayed, but briefly; then he stripped
Down to his shirt, and disposed himself for death.
But those two Friars, and a fellow of Brasenose
Who came with the crowd, never left off pestering
To make him change his mind. Until at last the chain was
        brought.
Then the Friars left him.
He held out his hand to those that were near,

But the Brasenose man would not take it. And then
The wood was set alight. And stretching out his arm
He put his right hand into the flame. And there he held it
Steadily, so that this hand of his was burned
Before the fire had reached to the rest of his body.
I am telling you the truth, and everyone could see it.
Still he stood, as still as the stake he was bound to,
Except that with his other hand he sometimes wiped his
   forehead,
And he murmured of *his hand, his unworthy right hand.*
Then, praying that Christ would receive his spirit,
In the greatness of the flame he gave up the ghost.

For a New Voice

For George Fraser

Muse of middle-age, ice on the wings,
   Earthbound looks toward skies
Where once she looped and curtsied;
   Or, hovercraft close to the ground, goes
   On a cushion of stale air,
The breath of bygone verses.
Too conscious of too much, waits
   For the irresistible moment,
   Through days, months, years, silent.

Each year a bird moults, new plumes
   For old acquires, new voice
   After the winter whisper;
And a boy before his manhood comes
   Breaks his old flute, is given
   The key of bass or tenor.

O Muse, who should be heavenly, break
   My voice, make me a new one!
Rid me of this old sound-box,
   Trap of exhausted echoes

And coffin of past power.
Make it anew, and now:
Not swan-like, in my dying hour
Only to sing in pain,
But now, a poet's voice again.

A Taste for Truth

For *miracle*, they say, translate *a sign.*
If God made water into wine
What was his meaning? That his laws
Are not immutable? Though our state is miserable
Yet all might live in glory if they chose?
Wine of our joy and water of our tears
Are not so incompatible as we think
If the atoms did not change, but those who drank.

In salt water our life began
And our blood is a salt solution.
We live upon this one condition –
Salt is good, salt is bitter.
All men born have wept salt tears,
All have wished to run from pain
And yet to live; all might learn
To love the sharp maternal brine
Could salt water taste like wine.

And if we say that we were foreordained,
All that expense of stars was planned
To bring self-consciousness to birth –
Megalomania? Well, we share our earth
With cousins vile enough, clever enough
To make us humble as regards our skill.
And yet, if spiders abash man's pride of life,
They make his charity seem more marvellous still.

No cost of stars could seem too great
To have made man's love: love pays for all.
Harder to think it pays the debt

For man's pain, man's fall.
A woman bears a child, and sees
His doom (her gift) to suffer years
Of hopeless struggle with disease.
Another must endure the cries
Of hunger, with no crumb to give.
And here the radiant face of love
Perishes in a deadly radiance
At the hands of brother men
And the impartial brain of science.

The miracles of science are so often
Just what one would not wish; but then,
God's miracle of the universe
On any view seems worse.
That one should say 'All shall be well'
Is yet the strongest miracle of all.

The flesh that formed us can divide
To form a cancer, and the strength
That held our weakness be dissolved.
Even she, whose affable wit denied
The inordinate, when she came to die
Endured rebellion in her body.
I cannot forget her dreadful sickness,
Nor reconcile within my mind
Her cheerful life, her cruel end.
Yet in her dying eyes I saw
Bright pain and love inseparable,
Part of the truth and ineluctable.

Gide, who forswore belief in God,
Died like a hero, keen to know
The truth of death, and tell it somehow.
Honour to him who rejects nothing,
Peace to all memories! for we too
Would work that miracle if we could:
To taste the truth, and find it good.

Sick Boy

Illness falls like a cloud upon
    My little frisking son:
He lies like a plant under a blight
    Dulling the bright leaf-skin.
Our culture falls away, the play
    That apes, and grows, a man,
Falters, and like the wounded or
    Sick animal, his kin,
He curls to shelter the flame of life
    And lies close in his den.

Children in patient suffering
    Are sadder to see than men
Because more humble and more bewildered:
    What words can there explain
Why all pleasures have lost their savour,
    Or promise health again?
Kindness speaks from a far mountain –
    Cannot touch their pain.

Beecham Concert

A lifetime goes to make this music.
The old body, bundle of bones
Wired together, barely flickers:
Least gestures, costliest pains –
And the sound burns alive from the stick.

Cellini hurled in table, chair,
All that would burn, to cast his metal.
The bronze was flawed despite his care.
But the will itself is inflammable here –
This furnace takes the soul for fuel.

So an old man beats time.
When young men beat, we have in mind
The visible world, and love, and fame;
Here nothing is real but sound,
And death is merely the music's end.

Life is a straw bridging a torrent.
Based on a straw the old man stands:
His style, classical; his dress, elegant;
(On either side the gulf is silent)
Darts of lightning in his hands.

Modern Love

In Almost Cinderella, *the author said, 'he had wanted to recreate for
adults the impact the story had upon children...Prince Charming...
begins to strangle Cinderella in a very stylised way as the clock strikes. It
is part of the mockery of the cliché of love at first sight.'*
See The Times, *7 December 1966*

That strong god whose touch made Dante tremble,
   Who made the sun rise and the stars fall,
      And could make saints of you and me for an hour,
   Now that the world is wise has lost his power:
      He was only a pantomime uncle after all.

'Love for another is simply the willing of good'[1] –
   True for the Middle Ages, a genuine thrill,
      But now such childish fancies are outgrown.
   This is the truth for modern, adult man:
'Love is simply the perfect wish to kill.'

[1] Aquinas

Three Sonnets

In Memoriam the Composer Robin Milford

I

I write no requiem, since rest you have
    After much torment; nor to compose a dirge,
Since death was your desire; but to bring alive
    These husky thoughts of you, as on a page
The seedling notes can quicken like the corn.
    Could I but speak you into life, so long
As the poem lasts, as I can hear reborn
    The passion which you planted in a song!

If poetry were music... but too dense
    Words seem for this, toneless, durationless.
    Unvalued the visions that a word can raise,
Unvalued the summer leaves and fruits of sense,
    Beside the sound, so thrilling, sad, concise,
    Of the robin's song on icy leafless days.

II

And myths are true: for wounded against a thorn
    You made your music. Why you should suffer so,
Being innocent, is more than myths discern,
    That help us, not to understand, but know.
Innocent, gentle, tormented, gay,
    The cause of joy in others – such was your nature.
Troubles that can be spoken do not slay;
    Therefore, till music failed, you could endure.

Lily-field freshets and bells of a Dorset valley,
    Blue lias and gold-capped cliff – O where, where
Is the resignation that we found in Hardy?
    Wild music of wood and heath that made endurable
    The griefs of man, and made that sorrow noble
Which seems in life an unredeemed despair.

III

To Justice on his calm impregnable peak
  Our cries hurl, our loss, our accusation:
That this should be the inheritance of the meek,
  To die self-tortured, in self-condemnation;
That music is no saviour to its maker;
  That the cause of joy in others finds no cause
To prompt his own rejoicing, and no succour
  Against the rack and flame of his own laws.

Reborn in a song... Our clamour dies away;
  The peak of Justice is unmoved and whole.
    Who shall measure a life's loss and gain?
Nothing atones. Only, through the skeleton tree
  A star looks, as an inextinguishable soul
    In the suffering body, irrelevant its pain.

Corneal Graft

And after fifty years of blindness
The hand of science touched him, and he saw.

A face was a blur, poised on a stalk of speech;
Colour meant simply red; all planes were flat,
Except where memory, taught by his learnèd fingers,
Spoke to his 'prentice sight.
                              As for the moon,
The Queen of heaven, she was a watery curd
Spilt on his window-pane,
For height, more than his stick could measure,
Was a senseless word.
The splendours of the morning gave no pleasure,
But he would rise at dawn to see
Distant cars and lorries, moving divinely
Across his strange horizon, stranger by far
Than the Pacific to the old explorers.

And is the patient grateful, subject of a miracle?

Blind, he was confident, forging through his twilight,
Heedless of dangers he had never seen.
As a dreamer on the brink of a ravine
Walks fearlessly, but waking, totters and falls,
So now the surging traffic appals him,
Monsters menace, he dare not cross:
A child, long past the childhood season;
A prince in darkness, but in the light a prisoner.

And if, after this five-sense living,
The hand of God should touch us to eternal light –
Not saints, well practised in that mode of seeing,
But grown-up babies, with a world to unlearn,
Menaced by marvels, how should we fare?
Dense, slow of response, only at the fingertips
Keeping some fragments of truth –
What could that heaven bring us but despair?

Mirror Image

When I look in the glass
    What creature looks back?
Not myself as I was,
    As I am, as I feel;
That face is not mine,
    Though reason declares
Soul and body are one.
    While my body was ageing
    What was I doing?
While cheeks grew hollow,
    While skin was coarsening,
    Eyelids drooping
    Where was I looking?

I looked at my friends
    And at you, my darling:
As a player who glances
Over his shoulder
    At Grandmother's Steps,

I knew you grown older
   Yet noticed no movement.
In you I engage
   The past and the present
In one bright image
   For ever true.

But while I watched *you*
   The girl in the mirror
Was making a face.
The self that I knew
   Is in focus no longer.
   'I want you to meet...'
My looking-glass says,
   And it shows me a stranger.

A Teacher's Funeral

You are present here:
Not *then*, not *elsewhere*,
But *here*, as we kneel, each seeing the same face,
Though inwardly, behind the eyes,
Deeper than the ear's echoes:
Five hundred insights of a single grace.

Single, but variously rich,
As differing in the share of each,
For memory in each has tender things to add;
And each (so confident now) once went
An urchin on those shoulders, bent
To carry children over their terror's flood.

It is no abstract image
That can for a flash our griefs assuage –
This inward touch of a true and loving presence;
As though our pain
Her self could summon
To share our narrow moment and our sense.

If ever earth's pull could make a current
In the heavenly element,
Surely thought so intense must make it stir;
If any pulse of finite love
Beats in the being that spirits have,
Our pulse beats gratitude, beats joy to her.

Thaw

The land takes breath; the iron grip
That clamped upon her heart is slackened.
On roofs the slithering snow-wrack
Like tods of sheep's wool slowly drips.

Earth's grey and foot-patched quilt of snow
Is wearing thin; the green shows through;
The carnival days of ice are gone,
The godlike skater's but a man.

As a sea-bird waddling on webbed feet
He is humbled; see him shamble
Clumsily up the hill, whose nimble
Swoops on the ice were a god in flight.

A curdled gravy chokes the gutters.
Yet on the lake the island glows
In crimson willow-twigs; the trees
Hold up the sky on bare, dark shoulders.

A Waving Hand

'...the need to reconcile the fact of what has occurred with the human imagination of it, to build up a sense of the past which is also a sense of the present...'

JOHN BAYLEY on Pasternak and Tolstoy

The death that we shall die
Is here, we know, coiled like a spring inside us,
Waiting its time.
When what is now becomes the past, we can see its future implied
As seed in the fruit, child in the womb.
The gardener, stooping down to tie
His bootlace, died so,
And acts through a lifetime multiplied
Foreshadowed this: when as a boy
He learnt to tie a bow,
Or when he stooped each day to dibble his plants,
Something was meant, he could not know.

So men seem walking histories
Of their own futures: we look to see the design
Forward or backward, plain,
As rings in a tree-trunk tell the sequence of years.
The jilted boy in pain
Trudging the pavement under the heartless stars
Now with his darling joyfully walks the same street.
Old words, old phrases, fly homing into the future
Where the poem is complete.

Parting a week ago,
The baby waved, through tears. I waved back lightly
With no foreboding fears;
But I remember it now,
And scan and search the memory, as though it should explain
All that came after, the anguish of last night,
The ambulance dash, the kind indifferent nurses,
And now the cot, where she lies in a hospital gown
And waves to me, through tears.

Suppose, when we are dead,
The soul moves back, over the gulf of nescience,
To relive a lifetime, all that was done and said ...
Some say remorse impels it, the pitiless conscience

That drives toward expiation;
But it might be a different need:
To live each *now* in the illumination
Of what's to come; wholly to understand
Those tears, that waving hand.

Winter Poem

November smells of rue, bitter and musky,
Of mould, and fungus, and fog at the blue dusk.
The Church repents, and the trees, scattering their riches,
Stand up in bare bones.
But already the green buds sharpen for the first spring day,
Red embers glow on the twigs of the pyrus japonica,
And clematis awns, those burnished curly wigs,
Feather for the seeds' flight.

Stark Advent songs, the busy fungus of decay –
They are works of darkness that prepare the light,
And soon the candid frost lays bare all secrets.

A Pirated Edition

Acquaintances
May meet and pass with a brief Good-day,
Yet each takes with him as he walks away
The other's image, lasting on like echoes,
Lingering like the print upon the retina
Of colour and shadow after the eyes close.

Phantoms criss-cross
Are sent from brain to brain, and none
Can call his straying image back again.
What part of me do you carry with you, friend?
Scraps of my speech, flashes of face and form
Unknown to me, that frolic through your mind.

And none can guess
How queerly he haunts another's dream;
How comic or how monstrous he may seem:
Royal personage prancing in cowboy dress
Or unjust judge – a pirated edition
Of his true self, and there is no redress.

'I Want, I Want'

Her body racked, her features crumpled
    Into a mask of woe –
This is Karen, two years old, forbidden
    Some trivial thing, I hardly know
    And she in an hour forgets what grieved her so.

Yet such intensity of sorrow!
    And the childless man who kneels
By his dead bitch, and babbling tries
    To call her back with desperate appeals,
    Who am I, to belittle what he feels?

Absurd to think all sorrows equal,
    And rate the grief of Lear
In the light of eternity no more than these.
    Yet these display what least and greatest share:
    The innocence, the sharpness of desire.

At Coole Park

'The woods at Coole... when I am dead... will have,
I am persuaded, my longest visit.'
W.B. YEATS: *Autobiographies*

The lady of the house is gone,
And nothing is left of it now, not a stick or a stone.
Contractors crumbled the heart away,
Leaving the rest to its vegetable decay.
And where the word was chief
There runs a wordless riot of stem and leaf.
Yet still the long enclosing wall
Held by the mothering ivy cannot fall;
And in the garden
Are widow's weeds, husks of life like a snake's skin:
Yellow-whiskered Rose of Sharon,
Traveller's Joy, Catalpa Tree,
And Box Walk
That leads to the Copper Beech, her visitor's book,
Where Yeats once set his mark;
Now scribbled over by Tom and Dick and Paddy.

Stranger, here pause,
And do not think to add your name to theirs.
You cannot buy immortality so.
But bend your soul to the touch of terror, know
At the sudden rushing sound
Of wings toward the lake that this is haunted ground.
Pray for this poet who spoke much,
And then beneath the scribbled Copper Beech
Sound the depth of silence,
Noblest monument for such a prince.

Too Much Skill

'When the artless Doctor sees
No one hope, but of his Fees...
When his potion and his Pill,
His, or none, or little skill
Meet for nothing but to kill,
    Sweet Spirit, comfort me.'
        HERRICK: *His Litanie*

Weeping relations in a ring
    Round the Victorian death-bed stand:
A public, but a gracious ending,
    Custom-propped on either hand.

Death with the faithful butler waits
    Just farther off, until the soul
Nods an agreement to the Fates,
    Keeping a vestige of control,

The end accepted like the start.
    Yes, even howls and funeral pyre
Assign to Death his ritual part;
    Only our age must play the liar,

Forcing the worn-out heart to hop,
    The senile to renew his breath,
Deploying every skill, to reap
    A few poor months of life-in-death.

Grant me an artless doctor, Lord,
    Unapt with syringe, mask, or knife,
Who when my worn-out body's dead
    Will fail to bring me back to life.

Islands of Scilly

For David and Alice Pennant

Dropping like gods from a cloudy sky
Into the jonquil fields the tourists come;
Then, with their sensible shoes, their County drawl,
Scatter as baby spiders out of a cocoon
And melt into the landscape. All
Hunt for the sun, and lay up gold in memory
From recollected daffodils, a hoard
Whose wealth alone plants people on these islands.

Circled by barren skerries, gushers of spray,
Breakers chafing its borders,
Here Tresco lays to heart a calm lagoon:
A tropic in a northern sea,
Where palm joins gorse, and the skin-deep-fertile land
Is pierced through with the jangling tones of ice-plants;
Stone garden in green waters,
With a comb of dark pines and skirt of dazzling sand.

A clutch of islands, every one distinct.
Yet these are fingers thrust to the sky
From a single fist at seven fathoms down;
And so our luckiest days
Rise from the dull, drowned mass of being
In brilliant peaks of joy.

Crab Signals

The Fiddler Crab waves an enormous claw:
    Tumescent signal of desire or hate,
    A summons and a threat.

This locked in battle is like an encumbered knight,
    Who by his heavy armour held immobile
    Can neither retreat nor kill.

The claw has a little, busy, tireless partner
  That forages round for eatable stuff, and then
  Hurries to scrape the monster clean

Of other lives that, given half a chance,
  Spreading like squatters on the passive surface
  Would settle and increase.

Scooping and scouring, it plays a Cinderella part,
  Wholly efficient to its purpose,
  And less absurd, for all its fuss

Than that monstrosity with the signals crossed,
  Or modern men who, bored with tenderness,
  Would bite as soon as kiss,

Would have all lovers raise the equivocal
  Claw-like banner of the aggressive will
  To capture and to kill.

Azalea in the House

This little shabby tree, forgotten all summer,
And crouched in its corner through December frost,
Now is brought indoors to keep its promise.
It speaks in a blaze, like a prophet returned from the wilderness:
The buds throw off their brown extinguishers, burst
Into flame, and March sees a midsummer feast.

Explosion of sunsets, archangels on a needle-point,
Red parliament of butterflies...
I cannot hold it with words, yet summer life
While winter howls out there behind the glass
And trees still clench their fists, must be too brief.

Scentless, infertile, kept from moth and rain,
Colour is its whole theme,
Like those vermilion rose-trees that bloom
In picture-books. They never drooped or faded,
But this has only a short month to shine,
And hours not spent in watching it are wasted.

Reading the News

Why does the story always turn out badly?
　In Bluebeard's castle now no rescuer
Comes to redeem the lost, no tears of pity
　Falling from heaven can melt the prison bar.

All these years we have watched the statesmen talking,
　The hopeful signing letters to *The Times*,
And while we dragged our feet, the road was leading
　To famine, torture camps, and atom bombs.

Heroes like Fischer, Grigorenko, face
　The worst of tyranny, while we fast bound
As in a nightmare cannot move a pace,
　And shout for help, but cannot make a sound.

Yet all art is not tragedy, and music
　Cries of a haven, over the storm swell.
Where did they find their faith, the serene masters,
　Their crazy word, that all shall yet be well?

Delphi

Finches in the Castalian stream
Wink a golden wing;
And the deep cleft, where steam
Could spiral into prophecy,
Contains a trickle of water and no mystery:
All the temples are open to the sky.

Arguing over the oracle
Tourists try to eat the plane tree's fruit,
Or choosing picture postcards try
To trap a moment's ecstasy.
All the temples are open to the sky.

Whatever stirred the Delphic seer,
Whether a god's whisper
Or fumes of cyanide as some declare,
No longer speaks. Mycenae is still red,
But with the poppies' blood.
Something remains yet to be understood,

Yet to be reconciled:
The lucid sculpture and the riddling darkness.

Our knowledge and our ignorance
Are brought to judgement here
Between the shining rocks and in the mountain's trance.
Blue the air and bright the stream
Where goldfinch fly;
Dark as ever the god's reply,
Though all the temples are open to the sky.

'Into the Whirlwind'

A documentary, suggested by
Eugenia Ginzburg's book

Here the peaceful flocks are grazing
    Over the green hill;
Lovers lie on a curly fleece;
    Wind wails and is still.
Now the sirens wail, and cease.
Europe trembles, but the siren
    Only called in fun.

And here the nightmare dread comes true:
    Torn from the fireside, whirled
Into the storm, to meet no more,
    Husband, lover, child,
In cell or camp, year upon year,
Now prove how Soviet tyranny
    Outdoes the cruel Tsar.

Those were the 'thirties. Growing in England knew
The common injocundities, the common
Tremors of adolescence, with its fear
To be found out, found wanting, never to be loved.
Surrounding us were the workless, mortified,
Shaming our youthful dilettante distress,
As now her chronicle of torment shames me.
All of us fearing war...
                          Fears were not liars,
For the day came when the sirens wailed in earnest;
Terror broke from the sky, as we knew it must.
A world ended.
                          And a world survived.

Now, as men creep from their holes, what hope
Lifts a faint arc, where the political prisoners
Toil from dark to dark, the deadlong day?
They live in the habitual present tense of pain:
Hope were a span too long to measure, only
Endurance counts, to survive until day ends;
To move, not fall; to live, for a crust of bread.
Life here is a stain in the snow from rag-bound feet,
A wisp of breath, faint as the Arctic sun
Too weak to rise, that lies low on the horizon.
How should the prisoner raise
Her heavy heart, whose only comfort is
That 'each day dies with sleep'?

But gentle sleep's a traitor too,
      For sleep renews the cells
To life, and another day's endurance,
      Though the heart rebels
Against its own absurd resilience.
Brothers, under the same sky,
      They suffer; we go free.

For here again the flocks are grazing
      Over the green hill.
What if the Nazi monster died?
      The heirs of Tolstoy still
Must stain the snow with liberal blood.
And still our lovers' peaceful scene
      Is cross-cut with their pain.

Some Time After

Where are the poems gone, of our first days?
  Locked on the page
Where we for ever learn our first embrace.
  Love come of age
Takes words as said, but never takes for granted
  His holy luck, his pledge
That what is truly loved is truly known.
  Now in that knowledge
Love unillusioned is not love disenchanted.

The Departure

The Departure, a one-act opera for two characters with music
by Elizabeth Maconchy, was given a Sunday evening
performance at Sadlers Wells by the New Opera Company,
conducted by Brian Priestman.

*Julia is sitting at the dressing-table in the bedroom, hurriedly
making up her face.*

JULIA

I shall never be ready in time.
Why, when one specially wants to hurry
Does everything choose to vanish?
My thoughts are all in a snarl,
My fingers are all thumbs.

How *plain* you look, poor girl!
Mark doesn't like me to rouge my cheeks,
But to-day I must, a little,
And now the rouge has vanished.
O, someone has hidden everything –
Nothing is where it should be.
Who would think that this is my own bedroom?
I feel like a stranger – a stranger even to myself

(The sound of voices chanting, and drawing nearer, is heard.
It is a funeral procession. She moves to look out of the window.)

May his soul find peace, whoever he was!
Whoever he *was*? . . . I talk like a pagan:
Whoever he *is*, whoever he may become,
Weightless beyond the burning margin of our air,
A stranger to us and to our ways of feeling
As I – yes – as I feel myself a stranger.

(She turns back.)

Even the room looks strange:
The bed – why is the bed not made?
Wasn't I here last night?
Clouds come rolling through my brain
And all my life seems hidden.
But Mark – I know he is coming,
And I must not keep him waiting.

Mark – O blessed, blessed name,
My frolic joy, my peace.
When he comes, it is May Day:
I shall be free, I shall be gay –
O let him not delay:
Return, return, my love!

But why is this? How strange it is –
I cannot see his face!
I cannot bring his face to mind.
You have been gone too long,
Return, return, my love!

(Footsteps and voices outside. She goes to the window again.)

You are coming, beloved. I had your face by heart,
But my eyes failed me. Now I see it with my eyes,
I see your face. And all these are our friends:
Why am I watching, not *with* you?
Here I am! Mark, look up, I am here!
He takes no notice. Mark! Can't you hear me?
Mark! It's useless, I can't make him look up.
He is shaking hands with them all. But what has happened?

(She turns from the window.)

Why are we not together?
He looked like a stranger. Someone looked through his eyes
Who would not smile if we met, someone
I do not know – someone I fear to know.
I wish we were safe in one another's arms
Housed in our love, and grief outside, like rain
That falls, and dies in the earth, gone like the dirge
I heard just now.

(The door opens and Mark enters.)

You are here at last, my darling!

*(She goes to meet him, but he walks straight past her and
kneels by the bed, his head buried in his arms.)*

A stranger, I said. You have my husband's form,
His walk, his look – ah, but not wholly his look . . .
Lift your head; let me see your eyes again.
Are you deaf and blind? Why don't you answer?
I thought we had been lovers once,
Had lain here together. Lift your head –
Turn, as once you turned in the Square garden
That lies like a green lake in the arid city,
Green in the tundra of the city streets.
Everything stopped for a moment – you remember? –
As though the policeman's hand, checking the traffic,
Waved it to silence, waved the birds to silence,
The spluttering engines and the clattering wren
All stopped as you turned to look,
And I walked on, till under the double cherry
As under nodding Venus, we met.

(He lifts his head.)

MARK

Julia! Are you trying to speak to me,
Or is it my longing that calls your voice from the air,
Sounding as when we met, under the cherry? . . .

JULIA
'Good afternoon,' I said, 'What a lovely day!'

MARK *(turning to her)*
Julia!

JULIA
      Unmerciful God –
I remember it now, in a flash: the car, the crash...
I died in that crash.
The stranger who looks from behind your eyes, it is Death!

MARK
Death? I saw you, dead,
Just now we laid your body in the grave,
Yet here you stand, exactly as I have longed to see you,
Have longed to embrace you...

JULIA
         No, never again.
I was waiting for you; I did not know that I was dead.
Where is that Death they paint, with the grinning skull
And gaping eyeholes? I should have recognized him there,
But how could I know him in you? They have not met Death
Who paint him like a monster:
He comes with the face that we love most.

BOTH
O, why did we go to drive that day?
Why did we choose that road,
And reach the spot, just at that moment?

O time, turn back, turn back,
Turn back to a safe day
Before the menacing morning,
And bar the door that leads to the dangerous road.

O time, turn back, turn back,
Turn back to a safe day:
Let us start on a different way,
And travel together the lime-flower lanes of peace.

JULIA

But no, it is I who must start, and travel without you;
It is I who must go.

MARK

Don't leave me!
Wait, Julia, remember our life together:
Remember the Summer Ball...

Your thistledown dress
That flew with the clock,
That tossed on the music
Like balls on a fountain;
The brilliant wine
Like stars on the tongue.

Our eyes full of love,
Our speech full of nonsense
With bubbles of nonsense
Like air in champagne,
And all the wide halls
Quite empty of pain...

JULIA

Long over, the Ball.

MARK

                        But our child lives still!
He lives; he needs you. For his sake, stay.

JULIA

I see him for ever:
His cradle set by a waterfall,
Wrapped in his shawl,
Our new-minted boy
On the green lawn of the mint-fresh river;
Hands that twirl as the river whirls,
Wordless speech like the gentle jargoning water.
I see him for ever!
But the river, not I,
Must sing his lullaby.
O, life is good, it is hard, hard to leave it.

MARK

Then do not leave it. Stay with me!

JULIA

You hold me back, yet it is you have taught me
What I must do, dear Mark.
Before you came
I only knew that I was not ready,
Hastily rouging my face, combing my hair –
Why was I getting ready?
O, not for you and your most sweet return:
It was my death that I was not prepared for.
We do not recognize death, coming so suddenly,
And we must know our death,
Or else our souls are imprisoned in the past.

MARK

Then, if the past will hold you near me,
So let it be. I'll share your prison,
We'll live in our past for ever.

JULIA

No, dearest, our joy has left those towers
And climbed before us; we must follow.
Joy is afar, over the Alps of loss.

(The funeral music is heard again.)

Hark, do you hear that?
Twice he has called me: now I begin to be ready,
I begin to understand his words.
He is saying, 'Part. Depart.'
O, Death is our parting,
Nothing else, and so he wears your face for me.
He is saying 'Part, Depart.
You have to depart alone,
And if to meet again,
That does not now concern you.'

MARK

But I hear nothing! Not a voice, not a word.
Where are you going? Do not leave me,

What shall I be without you?
A ghost chirping among the shadows.

JULIA

I am already far:
I am not what once I was.
Your face is no longer yours.
The being behind your eyes
Is neither enemy nor friend.
Behind your eyes is nothing now
But a bridge, over a black abyss,
A bridge, leading to darkness.
That bridge I cross.

MARK

Joy is afar, over the Alps of loss.
Julia, I am losing you!
Julia, I cannot see you!

JULIA

Nor sight, nor touch, only the word Depart.
Depart. Depart.

The Jesse Tree

A Masque with music by Elizabeth Maconchy
and stage design by John Piper,
was performed in Dorchester Abbey in 1974.

Characters

Peregrine (a girl)
Jesse
The Son/Baldur
Mary
Four Dancers
Chorus

*At the opening of the Masque, Jesse is lying at the
foot of the Tree, and the stage is in darkness. During
the Prelude, the light grows, and Peregrine enters
from the West end of the church.*

PEREGRINE *(on lower stage)*

I have come like a pilgrim,
But not to see the bones of a saint;
I have come a long journey,
But not to buy relief from pain.
I have come like a modern pilgrim:
Because I must be moving,
Because I belong nowhere.

Well, it was hot outside, and I was tired.
In a church you can rest – it's quiet,
The quietest place left in the world.

(She sits down)
Quiet – and yet I can feel them listening,
The silent crowd of the dead.
The trace of their lives is all around me,
Their bones lie under my feet.

(She moves to the Tree)
This is their house, not mine;
Their faith is nothing to me,
The church no home.
And this is not my family tree...

How lucky they were, the men who made this Tree!
They knew their place in the world,
And why they were alive;
The knew why evil came, and what could cure it.
The King of the Universe was their friend;
The stone arms were spread in blessing,
Bearing the wise Prophets, their uncles,
The holy Apostles, their brothers.
The stem grew from Man, the humble root,
To God-in-Man, the crown.

But that was a dream – only a glorious dream.
And now the line is broken, the throne is empty.

(She returns to her seat)
I'll sleep a little, then move on.
Only a dream... yet what began it?
Who made the Tree, who marred the Tree?

She sleeps, and the stage is darkened, the East window lit.

JESSE & CHORUS
Living men who learn of lives long ended
Feel themselves more strongly alive.
The words remind them they must die,
Yet here they touch the past, and seem to be
Branches of some growing tree.

(Mary's Voice off sings)
And so it grew and grew, and bore and bore,
Till at length
It grew a gallows and did bear our son.

Jesse moves to Peregrine, as the light grows on stage.

JESSE
Do not wake, yet see.
Open your eyes, yet sleep still.
See!
(Peregrine springs up)

PEREGRINE
Ah!... Who are you? *(She moves to run away)*

JESSE

Do not be afraid. I have come to answer your question.
For I am the root of all living things,
The base by which you stand upright.
I am Jesse, who lie at the root of the Tree,
And I am Atlas, bearing the weight of the world.
We belong to one another.

PEREGRINE
                    How can that be?
I am only a passer-by; no child of yours.

JESSE

Our history is a long one.
There are many ways of telling it,
But you have a part in all.

PEREGRINE
I have a part in all?

JESSE

Yes, branch of my Tree.
You ask, How can that be?
Wait now, and I shall show you.

*Momentary darkness, during which the Son takes his place in front of
the Tree. Light as of fire plays on him: he raises his arms and moves
them rhythmically as Jesse sings.*

JESSE

In the beginning was the fire,
And at the heart of the fire danced the creating Word.
The Word named the fierce beasts, the powerful atoms . . .
(Melismatic song for the Son)
So he held them in their chains,
That warring, whirling, they should keep their still
                                        unchanged relation:
The atoms' dance, the chemical constellations.
After the fire came the rock, then came cloud and water;
After the fiery red, the green;
Out of my body, a green tree.

Light effects as of leaves on the Tree.

CHORALE (I)

> On the world's hill stands a Tree,
> Finer than was ever seen:
> On that Tree there grows a branch –

Who

> has seen the blossom
> Growing, shining, on that Tree?

JESSE

This is the World Tree, Yggdrasil,
Connecting earth and heaven.
It moves and yet is still;
Its leaves die, and yet its life goes on.
All the unfettered spirits glide in its boughs,
All the passions of men course in its sap.

Its lord is the young god of light,
And round about it dance the elements,
Powers of Earth, Air, Fire and Water,
Knowing their movements and their stations,
Happy, supreme, serene.

During these lines the dancers representing the four elements enter; and now they dance. The Son remains by the Tree, and as they fall back at the end of the dance, Peregrine goes near to him.

PEREGRINE

What is your name, lord,
You who are the crown of the Tree?

THE SON

Baldur, the Bright God, is the name men give me.
I am the source of light.
This power is mine, that I can look away men's pain.
At sight of me, their sorrows wither, their tears are dried.
At my look, they laugh for joy.
And yet, one ill there is that I cannot cure,
For I have terrible dreams.
In my dreams, my light is quenched, I am drowned in darkness.

(As he sings, Loki and blind Hodur enter and crouch, watching)

CHORUS

The Bright God has evil dreams.
What shall be done to exorcise his dreams?

JESSE

Let the four elements pledge themselves.
Let them take an oath, never to harm him.

CHORUS

*(as the four dancers come in turn with outstretched
hand to touch the Son)*
Earth shall swear never to harm him;
Water shall swear never to harm him;
Fire shall swear never to harm him;
Air too shall take this oath.

JESSE

Now he is safe: nothing can harm him.
To prove the power of the oath, hurl at him:
Hurl at him, stone, wood, flame and metal.
Nothing can harm him.

*The dancers mime the hurling, the Son laughing. Then at a pause
in the game, he comes forward to front of stage.*

THE SON

Their shafts do not hurt me,
Yet still the dream haunts me.
(He sees Loki, and turns to Jesse)
There is no safety in an oath,
For on your Tree, O Jesse, grows
A plant that does not own allegiance
To earth, or air, water or fire.
If my enemy should find it
He could pierce my heart.

He moves back, and the mime is resumed.

PEREGRINE

There are two who stand apart.
One is blind – and the other does not play.

Loki begins to move from side to side of the Tree, searching.

PEREGRINE

The one who did not play is searching.
What is he looking for, hidden in the Tree?

JESSE

No! No! He must not find it!

PEREGRINE

Still he is searching...

JESSE

Hide yourself,
Hide yourself, mistletoe plant!

PEREGRINE

He is smiling...

JESSE

He has found it,
He has broken the deadly branch.

PEREGRINE

What will he do?

JESSE

The thing that Hatred longs to do.
But not by his own hand – he is too cunning.
He will not show himself.
A blind hand will deal the blow.

*During this, Loki moves behind Hodur and guides his hand
to throw. Baldur falls, and Loki steals out, but Hodur, not
knowing what has happened, stands laughing, while the four
Elements kneel with heads bowed, covering their faces.*

JESSE AND CHORUS

The young Prince has fallen,
The light is quenched.
All creation mourns him.

But Ignorance stands laughing,
Not knowing what his hand has done,
And Hatred stands triumphant.
Now Earth must cover her young lord's body.

CHORALE (2)
(as they carry the Son out, Hodur gropes his way out after them)

He is dead, his light is quenched.
Sorrow darkens all our world.
Lost to us his shining face
Lost
is all his beauty:
He is dead, and all must die.

PEREGRINE
O why, why?
Why must Perfection fall and die?
And why was enmity given the power to destroy?
Has history no place for a happy ending?

JESSE
I cannot see so far;
Because as yet the story has no ending.
Baldur is dead: you cannot weep him back to life;
Glory in his shape comes no more.
And yet it does not die,
But as a wintering creature wakes
At the sun's signal, so it shall come
In a shape more marvellous than was seen before.
Love is now to be born the son of man.
A tree now shall win back what was lost by a tree.

JESSE, PEREGRINE & CHORUS
A tree shall win back
What was lost by a tree.

*Darkened stage, light behind East window. Then the Tree is lit
again, to show Mary in her place, Jesse at the foot. The Angel
enters for the Annunciation, while the chorus sing 'Angelus
ad Virginem'. Then Mary comes down. She holds her cloak as
though sheltering the baby. Jesse stands behind her, as Joseph.*

MARY

Speechless stranger from a far land,
Bird of Paradise alighted on my hand,
    How can I deserve you?
Loving you first by faith, I love you now indeed;
Glory's best gift is its helpless need:
    Let me live to serve you.

JESSE

God has taken a man's way into the world:
Let us endow him with the gifts of a man,
Let him, receiving, make the gifts good.

*He calls the three Kings in turn from the wings; if possible
their gestures should recall the pledging of the elements.*

Bring him power, that power may be free of corruption.
Bring him knowledge, that knowledge may be free of arrogance.
Bring him grief, that grief may be free of bitterness.

CHORUS

Young beam of heaven, enclosed within
The lantern of a human skin,
How shall we face the full-blown light
Who find the bud too sharp for sight?

CHORUS

All the blessed lights of earth
Are little candles to his birth:
Too bright to bear, unless he could
Find means to make our weakness good.

PEREGRINE

Our darkness gives his light its place,
Our darkness gives a Prince his peace:
He puts his life within our hands,
And in that cradle sleeps, and shines.

The Kings rise and go out, as Peregrine continues to Mary.

These brought presents, as to a christening.
I have no present to bring:
Only my doubts, my restlessness, my longing.

MARY

You are here: it is enough.

PEREGRINE

Here, and now, I believe, I belong.
With my love I feel I can weave a warm
Shelter for the baby. But I cannot be always
Kneeling by his cradle. I shall go my way.
My head in a cloud of cares, I shall forget him.

MARY

He puts his life within your hands...

Faint chanting by the men of the Chorus: Where? Where?

MARY

And in that cradle...

PEREGRINE

     No, I did not mean it!
Not my hands – I cannot hold him safe.
Listen – what is coming? O, why did you bring him into the world?
Why did you trust us?

MALE CHORUS

Where, where, where?
Where are the children hidden?
Search them out,
Search the house, search the cradle –
Search in every corner,
Bring out your little ones, or we shall drag them out.
Bring out the children!

JESSE *(looking off-stage)*

They are hunting down the children!

PEREGRINE *(running to Mary)*

O, what shall we do? – Where shall we hide him?

CHORUS

None are to escape, we must kill every one!
Kill, kill! No mercy. Kill! *(Receding)*

JESSE
The hunt is passing by: the wolves have other meat –
Poor children – poor mothers! I cannot look.

CHORUS (*growing fainter*)
No mercy. No mercy. Kill every one of them!

PEREGRINE (*looking off-stage*)
It is past, thank heaven.

MARY
But it will come again.
For precious life is bought at such a cost,
And over against each joyful mother
There stands one weeping.

PEREGRINE
So the babies are dying in his place, they suffer
At his coming into the world.
Is the joy worth such a cost?

MARY
          How can I say?
For this is my hour of joy. While this time lasts
I am the universe to him, and the cure
For every sorrow lies in my love.
When he comes to his kingdom of charity and pain
I must be dethroned. I cannot heal heartbreak.

And now I hear the rustle of Time passing...
Even as I speak, he is growing away from me;
I shall forget what he was, how he looked –

She moves to the Tree and stoops as if laying down the child, her back to audience; then kneels, arms extended.

My son, you are leaving me.

Jesse and Peregrine move to upper stage, and stand on either side of the Tree.

JESSE
Like the great sails of a mill
The seasons whirl and swoop,
Sun and snow enliven the Tree.

PEREGRINE

The inner fire is glowing;
And through the coarse rough bark the delicate bud is forced.

BOTH

So he springs toward manhood;
So the boy is growing.

CHORALE WITH TRIO

Mary rises to join them. During the Trio, the Chorus sings verse I of the Chorale, 'On the world's hill stands a Tree...'
Look neither back nor forward –
Now is what matters.
Toil of the cells' dividing,
Leap of the quickening powers:
Thirty years that are hidden,
Three years more that are seen –
Three years, long as a life-span.
Look neither back nor forward:
Now is what matters, now...

The three come forward to the lower stage, and wait expectantly.

PEREGRINE

Now let him come, our Lord full grown.
Earth, sky, sea, fire and the hearts of men
Wait for his coming.
Let the King come to his own.

Chorus begins a mutter of doom.

JESSE

He is coming, child, but not as you thought.
Enmity, Ignorance – had you forgotten them?
These wait for him too.

The Son is dragged up the Nave by the Destroyers, followed by a crowd. Peregrine meets them on the steps of the stage.

PEREGRINE

Wait – why are you torturing him?
What evil has he done?

You do not answer.
Surely he must have done some terrible thing?
What was his crime?

All draw back a little, and silently point at him.

THE SON

I answer for them.
My crime is that I am.
Through my life, life is created.
Through my goodness, evil is ashamed.
They live, they suffer and do wrong:
They cannot forgive me this.
Because creation groans in anguish –

ALL *(speaking)*
Justice demands his death.

CHORUS
Death...

The Son moves to upper stage, meeting Mary.

THE SON
Mother...

MARY

My son. Was it all for this?
The long journey of your boyhood
Travelling from my arms, to this?
You were born to be king, I thought:
I gave you up to the world, too precious
For one to keep – was it for this,
A death on the gallows?

THE SON

Born to be king, yes,
And this my throne. *(He points to the Tree)*

MARY *(to the Destroyers)*

You cannot do it.
(Murmur from the Crowd) Think what you do

If you destroy a man. Think
How cherished is every living cell,
Bought at such cost of love and pain –
O, every inch beloved! You cannot
Cannot do it! *(Another shout from the Crowd)*

THE SON

    They cannot kill
The child you hold – you have him for ever.
Be comforted! I have accepted
What must come.

The Destroyers hustle him to the foot of the Tree,
and take off his cloak.

JESSE *(to audience)*

Yes, what a costly creation is a man,
So cherished in his cradle – every inch beloved!
And now that he is grown – listen,
Do you hear those cries of pain?
Martyr at the stake, scorched by religious fire –
Political prisoner, nails torn out, genitals pierced –
Jew in the camp, digging his own child's grave –
What has it become, this human form divine,
Every inch beloved?

The Son, scourged by the Destroyers, has fallen. He
staggers to his feet, and forward.

THE SON

Think – Is this a man?
Toiling in the mud,
Fighting for a scrap of bread,
Dying at a whim?

Is this a woman?
No hair, no name, no memory;
Eyes empty, womb cold
Like a frog in winter.[1]
Was man born for this?

He is dragged back, to mount the Tree, while Jesse continues.

[1] These lines are paraphrased from Primo Levi's book *Se Questo è un Uomo*

JESSE

After the camps, the atom bomb:
After Auschwitz, Hiroshima.
There in the distance, a cloud of a curious shape,
And here, the outline of a man, left on a burnt wall.
His shadow is all that is left of him:
The rest is now thin air – a poisoned air.

PEREGRINE

And this is done in my name. I cannot bear it!
I stayed safe in my home, and did not stir,
And now an invisible barrier holds me back.
I cannot reach him; I can do nothing.
I cannot bear it, yet I cannot prevent it.

CHORUS

Love dies, and let him die!

JESSE

And here, this creature, is this a man?
This scarecrow figure who cannot lie down.
He has been burnt with a special fire, that clings;
A fire so loving that it will not leave him.
They call it napalm.
Was this your son? You will not know his face:
His body has no skin.

THE SON *(on the Tree)*

On this tree of the world's life
I must suffer for that life.
For the evil done by bad men, knowingly,
For the evil done by good men, blindly,
I die willingly.
Because man did not choose to be,
And cannot say
If joy is worth the price he has to pay,
He must be revenged on me.

CHORUS *(while Destroyers and Crowd hurl at him)*

Love dies, and let him die.
Hurl at him – for his goodness is hateful.
Hurl at him – for the wonders he has done,

Hurl at him – for the pangs of birth.
Hurl at him – for the darkness of death.
Hurl at him – for his mercy endures for ever, and we reject it.
Love dies, and let him die.

THE SON
Tetelestai: it is achieved.

JESSE *(speaking)*
It is finished. He is dead.
Go now, for you have done what you came to do.

The Destroyers and Crowd go out.

MARY
He is dead! My dear is dead,
Stretched on our life's tree.
It grew to this, from the beginning of time,
Tall, from its tiny seed.
'And so it grew, and grew, and bore and bore,
Till at the length
It grew a gallows and did bear our son.'

CHORALE (3) *(while men and women come to kneel by the Tree)*
So it grew, and so it bore,
Growing still, and bearing still.
So it grew, and so it bore
Till
It grew, it grew a
Gallows and did bear our son.

PEREGRINE
Lord, these in their prayers accept the guilt
Of those who murdered you,
And ask forgiveness by their tears
For those who will not ask it of themselves.

(She goes to kneel by the others)
Forgive us also, who did not assent,
And yet did not prevent.
Turn back the world, to the place where all are innocent.

Since you have paid the penalty,
O let us start afresh, and be
As if we saw again the seed-time of the Tree.

TRIO AND CHORUS

Since you have paid the penalty
O let us start afresh, and be
As if we saw again the seed-time of the Tree.

The light fades as they end. Peregrine goes to the place
where she fell asleep; the rest go out, except Jesse, who
resumes his place at foot of Tree.

PEREGRINE *(waking)*

Either I slept,
Or else I was awake for the first time in my life.
The sights I saw
Are with me still, more vividly than daylight.
And you, stone Tree,
How glorious you were, and how ignoble!
I am a part of you:
I know that now; and now I must be going.
To start afresh! That was a wild saying.
But now I move, knowing myself to be
Actor in some great mystery,
Branch of a growing tree.

The Tree is lit. She walks out down the Nave.

Aria from A Passion Cantata

(Music by Bryan Kelly, 1993)

MARY SINGS AT THE CROSS

Hope sang at your cradle, son,
And every birth has Hope for midwife.
How was that lost? How can life
So cheat the promise of its opening,
Lost in the muddy shallows, that pure spring?

Was it for this I cherished you,
I fed, caressed your tender body?
Was it a lie then that I saw
In every perfect limb the sign
That the stuff of human nature is divine?

Now, bleeding and torn you hang
Whom I adore. I who could comfort
Every pain of infancy
Powerless watch you die, dear son;
Watch you endure extremity, alone.

Free Fall

In the year 1900, a French tailor proposed
to fly from the top of the Eiffel Tower in
a robe he had himself devised and made.
Film cameras recorded the experiment.

A long while, a long long while it seems:
The bat-winged figure shaking his robe,
      The cameras purring.

It is Daedalus the tailor, up on the Eiffel Tower
Ready to fly. The year is 1900;
      We watch it, now.

... Shakes at his bat-robe, first to the right,
Then left, then right again, a twitch,
      A doubtful gesture.

'Cast thyself from the pinnacle, angels will bear thee up.'
So great a height – the wings will surely beat
      And bear me up?

Shaking his robe. A mile of film we are wasting:
Why doesn't he jump? In these long seconds
      What is he thinking?

That the plan was crazy, and the careful stitches
Shaped him a shroud? Perhaps he is wondering
　　How to withdraw.

To pretend a flaw in the work, a change in the wind;
And imagines how it would be to face
　　The jeering crowd,

Slink back to his trade and live, with nothing to live for.
So still he hesitates, and shakes his shroud,
　　Then, suddenly, jumps.

Not even a flap from the wings. The lens below
Can barely follow the plummeting shape,
　　So quick his fall,

Hollowing out his own grave.
We are caught between dismay and laughter
　　Watching it now –

Not in a myth, not a century back, but now.
Ridiculous death. Yet as he stood on the tower,
　　Shaking, shaking his robe,

He mimed what each man must in private try,
Poised on the parapet of darkness –
　　Each in that crowd, and you, reader, and I.

Threescore and Ten

for Norman Nicholson

Praestet fides supplementum
　　Sensuum defectui

In every generation
The young acquire an image of their elders
Tranquil, assured, with every day mapped out
From punctual meals to reading by the fire.
Threescore and ten is not like that at all

We find on getting there. Life is not tranquil,
But someone else has come into the room
And looks at us from time to time.
                                    To admit
He's there is one thing, but the trick is harder
To welcome and ignore him. For it seems
The old should live as though their days were endless,
Yet also, feeling the glance of death upon them
Think that all time is Now, waken the power
Which looks athwart our days to what's immortal,
The Third Eye, which sees where sense is dark.

Didyma: Apollo's Temple

Yes, the camera can lie –
Do not believe it, go there.
Crouch in the shade of a column
To escape the burning sun
And know yourself diminished.
Men are pygmies here, the breadth
And height defeat their stature.
Thus the god should tower
Above his worshippers, although
Their muscles and their skill
Heaved up the blocks and smoothed the vault
With perfect ashlar facing –
Those craftsman-slaves, who scored
Their lord's initials in the stone,
Token of payment owing.

'Oui, on peut sauter' calls the tourist
Taking a short cut. Not for me:
Imagination's not so bold.
I cannot roof the temple
Or make the pillars march
The huge rectangle once they held.

Just as it fell the column lies
With giant overlapping drums
And measures what is lost.
'Ne peut pas sauter,' but
Gliding out of an ageless past
The kestrels, chestnut-backed,
And hoodie-crows contest the air;

Stone spiders on the wall and living
Lizards above the sacred spring
Confuse the centuries.
It is enough that here
A man feels small and takes
An exeat from his daily self,
To breathe warm airs, and see
Within the sanctuary
The dragon-arum's purple spadix.

'The lot of love is chosen'

W.B. Yeats

for C and K

But do you choose, or else does love choose you?
Our common speech, that utters mysteries
Only half known, insists we *fall* in love.
Who voyages on those seas
Goes to the ends of the world, a lifetime's journey.
Yet vows are chosen, and acts that make them good
Chosen, for better, for worse, or hard or easy.

I search for words to bless you, find none right,
But see that you from stores of joy already
Are blessing others, while your joys increase.
Blest be your chosen lot, dear son and daughter,
And the journey you began before you willed it –
Falling in love – upon those passionate seas.

2 October 1983

'The eyes looking out from our time-eroded bodies
are the lights of a soul that does not change.'
    THOMAS McFARLAND, *on chronology and Coleridge*

Years in the world threescore and ten,
And forty years of marriage.
Suppose the years together
Could now be known and gathered
In one intrinsic moment –
A drop of joy that, tasted,
Could still outlast the parting
Which all men must endure?
The moment of our meeting,
And this climactic birthday,
And all the times between?
Suppose – but we'll not linger
On this perennial prayer.
Once I recalled in a poem
Your hopeful infant snapshot,
And saw the gaze repeated
In the lover whom I cherished,
But could not see old age.
Seeing it now, I wonder
At the joyful mystery
That a man's life should age him
Yet leave him still the same,
And cherished, honoured, ever.

Red Square

Grim heads in a row
Above the mausoleum,
Enduring while the tanks roll by,
The world sees. The tourist,
Reckoning up the gilded domes
Under a cloudless sky
(All that investiture of light
On sprouting gourds of bright St Basil),

Bewildered, cannot marry
The evidence of what he knows
To the evidence of sight:
Shapes of a toy city,
The sun-washed, guilt-soaked, Kremlin.

Open House

For Winchester Cathedral Centenary

Churches are best for prayer, that have least light
John Donne

But then, why build a church at all
Or dream of glory, when to crawl
Into a hole could serve us better?
Where each in a private mist and utter
Silence may tread the whorling path
To find God at his being's core.
And Grecian temples we admire
For lightness and lucidity
Roofed by the blue and sunny sky
In their true form were close and murky.

Alone, then, to the Alone –
Dark oracle, or bloody stone?
Cathedrals take another way:
Like plants, and phototropic, they
Spire toward heaven, learn from trees
The branching vault, and canopies
Of fretted space. The ecstasy
Of power is here, coiled like a spring,
A god's mysterious gaiety,
And peace that passes understanding.

And this is home to us, although
Our numbers break its calm, we pry
With flaccid curiosity
And stray about on weary feet.
We are not much to boast of, yet

Thinking of God men built this home
And signed the work with man's own name.
Bracing their word is, and austere,
Admonishing our weak despair:
'Renew all hope, who enter here.'

The Runaway

Barnard's Star, a faint red dwarf at a distance
(from Earth) of only 5.9 light-years...is not
moving steadily. It is weaving its way along, and
there can be no doubt that it is being perturbed
by an invisible companion.

from an article by Patrick Moore

Barnard's Star is coming towards us
At sixty-seven miles a second.
Five years the light by which we see him
Travelled to reach us. Barnard's Star
Is moving drunkenly, led astray
By an invisible companion.
His other name – The Runaway.

Runaway Star when Christ was born,
No visible light has crossed two thousand
Years of time to show you plain,
And every year you grow more distant.
Yet on a word we travel back
To meet that orbit,
And the hero of that story
Like an invisible companion
Deflects our course, perturbs our days.

High Bield, Little Langdale

for Delmar and Josephine

The stillness of that valley
To town-bred ears is positive as a sound.
At early light the tarn
On dark-green glass re-prints the slaty mountain,
And little grassy hills
With rounded slopes follow each other in canon.

If there is sound, it is sudden:
Flycatcher clacks, robin winds an alarm-clock,
Or flings his chain of silver notes
Out of the yew-tree; then in the distant quarry
A wheel screams, slicing at stone,
Where sombre Wetherlam shows his frown-marks eastward.

Bright image on the remembering eye,
Your mountains go with each of us departing,
And traverse England; so for me
A winter long they loom in summer plumage.

But you, with a remembering brush,
Live for them, set all seasons on your walls, your heart.

Infelix Dido

Ille dies primus leti primusque malorem
causa fuit . . . (Aen.IV.169)
(That day was the first of death and the first
cause of woes . . .)

In a cave, safe from the storm,
Dido coupled with her love.
Nymphs shrieked on the mountain-top,
Lightning flashed and earth sustained
The piercing javelins of rain.
'That was the day sorrow began.'

Virgil blamed her it seems, for love is the foe of decorum.
All her generous hospitality counts for nothing:
Welcome given to beggars, the shipwrecked penniless Trojans,
Shelter provided, a share in the kingdom, while their leader
Prays the gods to reward her, if justice rules in heaven;
Prays that she may be blessed as she is prodigal in blessing.

> 'How could I help but fall in love?
> Bursting from the cloud your beauty
> Seized my heart, your history
> Melted all my soul in pity.
> Why could not your destiny
> March to one end with my desire?'

That is all irrelevant, the poem seems to be saying:
Things are as they are; the order of heavenly justice
Takes no account of the debt he owed, of pity or anguish,
Pays no heed to the irony when Aeneas asks a blessing.
She was entrapped by a god? So much the worse for her.

> 'Was not ours a marriage bed?
> Jewelled sword I gave you, purple
> Cloak you wore for me – my passion
> Woke an answering fire in you.
> Winter-long that torch was burning:
> How could you say it was no marriage?
> How could you say you gave no pledge?

> 'For such a wound there's no forgiveness.
> Though you declare your heart is wracked
> You yield too swiftly, follow your fate
> Too willingly. My only solace
> Since my desire is turned to hate
> Is that in dying I can curse.'

Fame and success for him, who obeyed with such alacrity,
And dared not tell her the news, but let her heart divine it.
Death in despair for her, and the epithet *unlucky*.
Yes, but the poem brought revenge, for Virgil's genius –
Whether he knew it or not – pronounced in Dido's favour:
Type of all tender hearts deceived, of prodigal givers
More loving than belov'd, and by their love betrayed.

Night Watches

Somnus lies on a couch of feathers,
Curtains, black, around his head
And dreams beside him. Breathing quietly
Lie the lucky who share his bed.

They in a moment cover the hours
From night to morning; but the rest
Deep in the gulf must feel their way
From hour to hour, with lids shut tight
On anxious eyes, groping alone
Toward a distant thought of light.

Friendly Somnus, show me the gate
Youth took for granted; now I am old
Let me not count those endless hours
Till time is short again, and day
Recalls with half-incredulous pain
The caverns of such a long, long night.

Requiem

for R.C.B. 1905-83

Lichen coats the pear-tree bark,
   Sap must still make shift to rise.
   Under skin a touch will bruise
Blood commutes in ceaseless journeys;
   Occult word that gives release
      Never conscious mind has spoken.

The animal is fain to die,
   The soul prepares an end, but still
   A hidden tyrant thwarts the will.
Yet he must yield, we know, though none
   Returns to share the secret, tell
      How at the last his power was broken.

Patient face upon the pillow
We have seen our last of you,
Yet have not taken leave; we find
Loss brings the subject closer, as
The telephoto lens
Distorts perspective, images
From far ago crowd on the mind.

You rise immortal there, although
The curtains slide across and hide
The bier that bears you to the fire.
A boy, a man, behind the eyes
Of every grieving face
Freely moves with a frolic life,
Multifarious, debonair.

It wakes our longing, brings no comfort,
Yet with a kind of joy attests
We loved no phantom. All will see
The jaunty beret, quizzical smile.
I add an impatient candid boy
Who seven years before me climbed
To the platform in the cedar tree.

But later days' humiliation,
Helplessness of once-proud flesh,
Tormenting clamour in the brain –
These I would forget, dear brother.
Yet through them I perceive
The shining of your valiant patience.
So, dark outlines, they remain.

Charles Williams: In Anamnesis

'That which was once Taliessin
rides to the barrows of Wales'

This is a likeness but it does not speak.
   The words are echoes, the image looks from the wall
Of many minds, kindling in each the spark
   Of passionate joy, yet silent in them all.
Pupils grow older, but a long-dead master
   Stands where they parted, ageless on his hill.
The child grows to be father of his father,
   Yet keeps relation, kneels in homage still.

What is the speech of the dead? Words on a page
   Where Taliessin launched his lines of glory
   Capture for him a poet's immortality
As every reader wakes them. So the image
   Speaks through a living mind, as he in life
   Would use from each the little that each could give.

Azizur

(A ten-year-old Bangladeshi boy, whose
mother was learning English from me.)

Brown boy, quicksilver glance, dark thatch of hair,
Orphaned of the warm Ganges,
Adopted son of our chilly white-willowy Thames,
Where can we meet, except in the Tower of Babel,
What pleasures can we share?

My life, my likings, are unresonant to you
As dolphin-talk to human ear,
And yours to me are not much clearer.
I must discard the image of my sons, while
Well-brushed, sedate, with an orange tie,
In Blenheim Park you plod politely by me,
Smiling, but tired in a half mile.

You are your parents' word-winner,
Earning for them the precious coinage of speech.
You guide your mother's finger over her primer,
A fragile bridge between
The bright voluble India of home
And the world where she is dumb.

Smiles, plentiful smiles we share,
And the wish to give, and the sunny taste of a mango.

Wentworth Place: Keats Grove

The setting sun will always set me to rights...
                    KEATS, to Benjamin Bailey

Keats fancied that the nightingale was happy
Because it sang. So beautiful his garden,
Behind the gate that shuts the present out
With all its greed and grimy noise,
I fall into a like mistake, to think –
Because there are such depths of peace and greenness,
Greenness and peace, because the mulberry
Invites with arms supported like the prophet,
Because the chestnut candles glimmer crimson –
That heartache could not flourish among these flowers,
Nor anguish resist the whisper of the leaves.

Angry for him, blessing his gift, I accuse
The paradise that could not save him,
Sickness and grief that sunsets could not heal.

Occasional Poems

1. LINES TO A RETIRING PRINTER

White limestone chunks from Flamborough Head
Whose curious eyes – deserted homes
Of immemorial creatures – now
Wink at me from the flower bed,
Remind me that the ceaseless cry
And whirl and sweep around the headland,
Turmoil of gull and auk and gannet,
Still goes on, though I'm not by.

So think, on pearly summer mornings
Tasting your freedom, think how still
The whirl and sweep goes on without you.
Tired committees gasp for air
While the Chapels issue warnings –
And you not there, and you not there!

2. UNSOLICITED CONTRIBUTION

Dear Madam:

I am a warm admirer of your work.
(This means – one poem, in an anthology, but
No need to mention that.) So now I send
Some poems I have written. I shall be glad
Of any comments you may like to offer
(Assuming these are favourable). Give me
Your honest opinion (this means praise, of course).

Since poetry's in question, I am sure
You'll not expect acknowledgement or stamps.
I may not be a Milton, and inglorious
Up to the present time I am, but mute
I certainly am not.
                         And so, expecting
Your helpful comments at an early date,
I sign myself
                Yours truly,
                         Aspirate.

3. TO TOM AND JEAN GRIFFITHS,
WITH A PHOTOGRAPH ALBUM

Here is the record of a winter's morning,
  Proof positive that we, and you, were there:
  Well-wishing friends, and one beloved pair.

What it could see, the camera faithfully told.
  It could not see, but we who know can tell,
  What made this home a haven for us all,

Where Welcome kept the door, Delight the table,
  Laughter attended; Kindness crowned each guest
  A king, and later cradled him to rest.

Song to Mark a Boundary

for the Blands at Augop

In these tall trees warbler and wren all day
Beat boundaries of music, marking a province.
The song of birds is functional, they say:
This year at least its function is delight
For you in a new-built house, here tasting a first May.
The notes seem colour of spring made into sound:
Viridian leaves of beech, and powdery gay
Yellow of hornbeam, all that your window sees;
Green slopes and golden kingcups for the play
Of evening light, where the obedient trees
Compose a parkland picture; far away
The hills of Radnor Forest – I name them yours,
For the eye possesses what it can survey.

New come, and well come now to the birds' kingdom
This mortal nest – newcomer but no rival.
My poem too is functional: I sing
To claim your territory, and to pray
A blessing on your house, and on your stay.

Immigrants

The Scandinavian *corps de ballet*
Usurps the lawn.
Twists and turns display an elegant
Slate-gray back; in speckled brown
And slashed with scarlet, smaller rivals
Move into place.
Sallying and retreating trace
An intricate figure in the snow.
The fixed points are fallen apples,
Hunger the choreographer.

Flutter and squabble disturb the surface.
All at once
Fieldfares abandoning the contest
Fill the trees like winter fruit.
A solitary mistle thrush
Arrives to scour the empty skins;
Redwings brood
As though the snow were a warm nest.

Cruel winter, friendly to me,
Accept my thanks.
Starvation and the snow combine
To bring me glory:
Watching the visitants, I exult
And think them mine.

Bempton Cliffs

For Richard Wilson

Strangely quiet, the cliffs are, as we approach.
The sea swallows the sound until, suddenly,
As though a door were opened into a hall
(A prayer meeting, a gaggle of gossiping talkers)
It's there, around us. And the sky in shreds
With whirling birds.

Now I am earthbound in a city of fliers,
A rooted maypole, while about my head
The dancers weave their patterns, maypole ribbons
Of varying flight, and their incessant cries
Are skeins of sound, flung up into the air.

Law rules the dance; in all these comings and goings
None is aimless. And all comparisons –
Comic, anthropomorphic – that spring to mind
At the sight of guillemots, tier upon tier
In dinner-jackets, like a festival chorus,
Are out of place.
                              Comparisons anyhow
Die in astonishment when we reach the cliff
Where the great ocean birds are perched.

That was no tractor you heard, but the gannets' talk.

The gale-masters, precipitous plungers,
Brood here on their scraps of net
With smaller birds around them, Viking beak
With its armoured look, subdued for a mating kiss,
Domestic as a farmyard goose;
So close, it seems as though a hand stretched out
Could touch and stroke the saffron head.

Jynx Torquilla
A Spell in the Air

In sallow winter days I remember
Jynx, jynx, the wryneck's call.

Not as the cuckoo's mate, but an August passenger
Blown off course, perhaps,
It stopped by, the husbandman's reward
For leaving ânts about in the garden.

Its head, as though on stretched elastic,
Wobbled slightly as it flew
(The neck, they say, writhes like a snake in courting).
Its plumage, colour of gnarled bark
Speckled with lichen,
And sticky tongue, lethal to ants,
Were ours to watch, while the feast lasted;
Then it took off, for Africa.

Jynx, jynx, I heard you cry.
For this, witches would catch and bind you on a wheel
To draw the souls of men on invisible threads,
And turning, screeching, with your spell –
Jynx, jynx –
Recapture faithless lovers.

Craig yr Aderyn: Bird Rock

*(A crag some six miles from the sea,
near Towyn in North Wales)*

To each, his memory of Eden.
For us, the sinless, cloudless garden,
And for these cormorants the lulling
Lashing waves of the wild sea.

Ages ago the sea retreated:
Still they build as their parents nested.
Memory holds the generations
Where no waves beat, no salt spray.

Their tall cliff has meadows lapping
About its base. Flapping their wings
They rise like ducks, but under water
Chase their prey with powerful feet.

Marine, and land-locked. Paradisal
Memories, or else ancestral,
Weave a complexity of being:
Always homing, never at home.

Viscum Album

Nothing in my year was stranger
Than your abrupt epiphany.

Searching where late windfalls lay
I looked up and you looked down –
Eerie web spun from the bough,
Green claws like thumb and finger,
And in the crook, a trinity
Whose pearly globes with glue betray
The gardener bird by whom they're sown.

In your cortex I should see
The bright god slain. It is no wonder
Churches would not let you enter.
Yet you are known for healing too,
Wood of the cross, our loss, our gain.

Parasite and prize to me,
Prosper in this apple tree,
And bless our lovers, mistletoe.

Mistletoe berries crushed make bird lime.
A mistletoe dart killed the god Baldur.
For each kiss under the bough a berry
is picked; when there are no more, the
kissing must stop.

Helleborus Niger

'There may have been a time, and there must still be a
place for H. Niger to live up to its name, Christmas
Rose.'   ALAN BLOOM, *Perennials for your Garden*

'Now in the time of this mortal life...'
The Saxons called it 'first of the year':
This should be the destined hour
To open, shining by dark leaf,
Christ's wintry flower.

Now is the time, and named for this
The Christmas rose.
But like the promised joy, it lingers
Under the ground, and still delays,
However the famished spirit hungers.

'Now in the time of' – but late in time
Christ's humble coming. Only wait:
The rose will not cheat belief.
We'll not re-name it, though so late
Its pure, gold-centred crowns unclose.

Snakeshead Fritillaries

Some seedlings shoulder the earth away
Like Milton's lion plunging to get free,
Demanding notice. Delicate rare fritillary,
You enter creeping, like the snake
You're named for, and lay your ear to the ground.
The soundless signal comes, to arch the neck –
Losing the trampled look –
Follow the code for colour, whether
White or freckled with purple and pale,
A chequered dice-box tilted over the soil,
The yellow dice held at the base.

When light slants before the sunset, this is
The proper time to watch fritillaries.
They entered creeping; you go on your knees,
The flowers level with your eyes,
And catch the dapple of sunlight through the petals.

Heliotrope

Helio-trope, turning towards the sun,
As I turn to you, today and always, beloved.
I put the plant in the ground for our wedding date
Although we forgot to recall it.
But the flower is only an annual, so next year
I'll plant another, to celebrate
Our perennial love.

The Surprise

This year, for Christmas star I'll choose
No spangle in the sky, but rather
An earthly one – if the frost spares it.
Turquoise berry
Centred in a magenta star,
Strange fruit of the clerodendron.

White summer blossom, sickly-scented,
Held this secret, was preparing
This surprise to outlast the leaves,
A cool blue eye to startle darkness.

Traherne and the Long-Legged Spider

'Love . . . is of all sensibles the most Quick and Tender;
being able to feel like the longlegged Spider at the
utmost End of its Divaricated feet.'
                                            Centuries IV.80

But for what purpose does the spider use
Its wary feet? For lightning-quick response
To lightest touch upon the web; at once
The prey is found and parcelled. This as an image
For Love's fine sensibilities disturbs.

Yet there's no inconsistency; no curbs
Constrain the single vision of Traherne:
Eternity in all appearances,
The holiness of everything that is.

Pain clouds the bright reflection; there remain
The immortal wheat, the temporal joy, to prove
How faithful is that doctrine, speaking of Love.

'Animula, Vagula, Blandula'
(After a Baptism)

Choir, candles, kindred faces,
Isobel goes in a gaggle of children,
'Issued from the hand of God'
To a plentiful drench of holy water,
Unprotesting, unperturbed.

Tiny chrysalis, lapped in shawl,
So parcelled, signed, and answered for.
But heart to heart against my shoulder
What I hold is something different:
Life beating with secret purpose;
What I see, face to face,
Is recognition,
Spark of the eternal light.

On 'The Glance' by George Herbert

'When thou shalt look us out of pain'

God's laser-look. The heart-struck pains
Of all our world shrivel to nothing?
Darkness cannot comprehend it.

As when through blackest clouds a beam
Strikes and illumines a single favoured
Golden spot. This for a token.

Or infant-gaze, fixing a stranger
Eye to eye, searching the core
To find a secret that's unspoken.

Joy was intended at our beginning.
Intense the gaze that probes this meaning;
Strong the soul that can sustain it.

Something Else

'They call it quiet affection. It's not affection, and it's
not at all quiet, but let that pass...'

CHARLES WILLIAMS

For V

Old age has its particular season,
Not quite to be compared with autumn or winter:
Not to the luxuriance of autumn,
Not to the austerity of winter.
Passion it has, compounded of present joy
And memory of past fulfilment;
Precarious, being timebound,
With pleasure the more poignant, so,
Its durable fire burns a lifelong day.

I might choose, for an emblem of its happiness,
The surprising glass-blue berry, held in a magenta star,
Of the fruiting clerodendron.

Villanelle for the Colour-Conscious

The world you see is not the same as mine.
Hue once meant *form*: you shape it differently,
And yet we both describe the same design.

The rainbow's tints are seven and not nine—
We need more terms to apportion what we see;
The choice you make is not the same as mine.

Travelling through the spectrum, we assign
The frontiers differently: what's green to me
Looks grey to you. Yet it's the same design.

Colour of flesh was once incarnadine;
Since Shakespeare, that's blood-red. In poetry
The world you see should be the same as mine.

Cyan, the Greek for dark-blue, we assign
To greenish-blue. Do we then disagree?
Or rather both describe the same design?

Some words arranged in order on a line
Are prose to one, to another, poetry.
The world you see is not the same as mine.
And yet we both describe the same design.

The Halcyons

How Ceyx, son of Lucifer, and his wife Alcyone,[1]
daughter of Aeolus, were changed into birds
OVID, *Metamorphosis XI*

1

Gently the waves
   On winter seas
Dandle the nest
   Through the calm solstice.

While storms menace
   A smooth dark space
Opens on furrows
   That dip and arise.

But by what sorrows
   Such peace was won
Is the bird's secret,
   The bright halcyon.

2

'Not over the sea, my love, do not set sail over sea,
For the winds are pitiless; I heard them in my childhood
Howling through my father's caves. If you must go
Let the journey be over land.' So Alcyone begged,
But gentle Ceyx, son of the morning star, would not listen,
Dearly though he loved her: disasters and portents,
A brother's fearful fate, robbed him of his rest:
He must consult the oracle, peregrine over seas
To understand the meaning, discover the remedy.
'At least take me with you, or I shall believe
I am dearer to you absent,' Alcyone said smiling.
'It is the loss of you, not suffering, I fear.
All is joy, if shared with you.'
           'Then send your heart with me,
And keep your body, that I worship, safe for me on land.
I swear I shall return.'
           Foreboding on the shore
She waves goodbye. The oars are double-banked, the hoisted sail

[1] I pronounce it to rhyme with 'Hermione'.

Soon drops below the horizon. Then begin the counted hours,
The empty days; the only solace picturing
His dear return, his arms around her – that and a faithful prayer
Each day to Juno; incense burnt, and candles lit.
But while she prays, a storm has caught his ship; mountainous
    waves
Crash on the deck, the mast is gone, oars and rudder smashed,
The captain's frantic shout unheard in the howling of the wind.

The ship shudders: now a hulk she lifts to a dizzy height
Then plunges sideways; all are lost in the writhing boiling water,
And Ceyx in the sea's throat calls out your name, Alcyone.

Even the pagan gods are not so heartless as we think them:
Hopeful prayers, where no hope can be, disturb the Olympian
    peace.
So, that Alcyone may know the truth in a true dream,
Juno summons from the cave of dreams Morpheus the son of
    Sleep
Who can assume all human forms.
                    Into her sleep he came
As from the sea, the water streaming from his hair and beard.
He seemed alive, as visions do, and yet she knew him dead.
'Precious Alcyone, your tears are all you owe me now,
For I am drowned. Your prayers could not turn aside the storm
Nor pacify the hungry seas. While I could I called your name
Until the waters closed over my head.'
                    She sprang to clasp him –
Poor naked ghost – embraced the air, and crying 'Take me with
    you,
I cannot live,' ran to the shore, as though the sea that stole him
Might hold him still . . .
            So far the story might be yours or mine:
Parting, death, and a revenant in dream; but this is fable,
And winged beyond our common skill to master fate.

As dawn broke she gazed over the dreary rolling waters
And saw far out a shape – was it a boat, was it a corpse?
Nearer and nearer it came, and as a wave lifted it high
She knew her husband's face, and knew that he fulfilled
His promise to return. At once, frantic to reach him
She ran to the little jetty, leapt, flew into the sea.

Changing as she flew, she uttered harsh sounds,
And reached him, a bird. The kisses of that bird's beak
Renewed his spark of life; intensity of longing
Drew him alive to share her nature.

So the life they share
Is not the life they lost, yet, always together
They mate and rear their young. In the winter solstice
Her father Aeolus locks up the winds;
While she broods, men call it the kingfisher weather.

3

When misery is greatest
    Souls take wing,
Feathered by desire
    Or despair, rejecting
Intolerable fact,
    Take flight into madness
Or die by their own act.

Away into the sky
    From the squalor of Milan
The luckless children fly
    In de Sica's film,
    As though to affirm
That there is no solution
    For life's cruelty,
    Only to fly away.

But something more is meant
    By those myths of bird-changes.
That love continues blest
    In different guises;
That immortality
    Is not mere repetition:
It is a blue flash,
    A kingfisher vision.
It is a new-feathered
    And procreant love,
Seen where the halcyon
    Nests on the wave.